The Political Economy of Antitrust: Principal Paper by William Baxter

A Liberty Fund Seminar
Administered by
The Law and Economics Center

The Political Economy of Antitrust: Principal Paper by William Baxter

Edited by
Robert D. Tollison
Virginia Polytechnic Institute
and State University

LexingtonBooks
D.C. Heath and Company
Lexington, Massachusetts
Toronto

The Political Economy of Antitrust: Principal Paper by William Baxter presents papers from a seminar held at the Law and Economics Center in October 1979 as part of the program of Liberty Fund, Inc. Liberty Fund is a foundation established to encourage study of the idea of a society of free and responsible individuals.

Library of Congress Cataloging in Publication Data

Liberty Fund, inc. Seminar on Political Economy of Antitrust, University of
   Miami School of Law, 1979.
   The political economy of antitrust.

   "Administered by Law and Economics Center, University of Miami School
of Law, Coral Gables, Florida."
   1.   Trade regulation—United States—Addresses, essays, lectures.
2.   Antitrust law—United States—Addresses, essays, lectures.   3.   Industry and state—United States—Addresses, essays, lectures.   I.   Baxter, William F., 1929- II.   Tollison, Robert D.   III.   Miami, University, of Coral Gables, Fla. Law and Economics Center.   IV.   Title.
HD3616.U47L49   1979   338.8'0973   80-7928
ISBN 0-669-03876-8

International Standard Book Number: 0-669-03876-8

Library of Congress Catalog Card Number: 80-7928

Contents

Preface

When government intervenes in the economy to regulate a private economic activity, legislators and government officials typically pronounce their actions as being in the "public interest." Modern scholarship in law and economics has pierced this rhetorical veil in case after case of economic regulation to ask the questions: which public, whose interest? In the process of answering these questions, the real economic basis of many regulatory policies has been found to be the excess returns that are inherent in these policies for certain well-organized interest groups. Trucking firms support entry restrictions in the interstate trucking industry, industry seeks environmental regulation in the form of standards rather than taxes, the major television networks strongly resist the idea of new networks, and on and on, ad infinitum. This is not to say that government regulation is a simple process to understand or that economists and lawyers have an adequate understanding of these processes at this point in time. The outlines, however, of a theory of economic regulation are clear. Regulatory intervention in the economy is fueled by the ability of some groups to obtain excess returns and misallocate scarce resources by means of legislative and bureaucratic fiat. The costs to the rest of us of this activity, while generally not large enough to provoke any one of us to seek to "deregulate" the economy, are large and growing.

As economists and lawyers have expanded the application of this model to explain government action, some areas of government regulation have remained unexamined. Antitrust is prominent among these areas. The general conception of antitrust law and its enforcers is that they protect us from monopoly. Scholarly interest in antitrust has traditionally been concerned with ways to make antitrust policy work better in this sense of protecting us from monopoly, that is, how antitrust can contribute to economic efficiency and to generally recognized principles of equity in the economy. These largely normative studies of antitrust issues are often supplemented by histories of antitrust, but these histories are typically stories without a model. Rarely has anyone framed a positive analysis of antitrust by asking, simply, what antitrust does.

In the central paper in this volume, William Baxter raises this fundamental question about antitrust, and, moreover, he raises it in the form of a testable hypothesis. Which public and whose interest does antitrust serve? Baxter argues forcibly that the primary function of antitrust is the protection of small businesses from larger and more efficient competitors, and he presents some convincing evidence in favor of this basic hypothesis.

This positive economic approach to explaining antitrust activities is a bold departure from conventional scholarship in this area, and, predictably, the commentaries on Baxter's paper by Harlan Blake, Yale Brozen, Kenneth Dam, and Oliver Williamson challenge his central thesis strongly. Moreover, the prepared papers led to a vigorous discussion among the invited participants—an edited version follows the papers. In addition to the points raised by Baxter and the commentators, the discussions raised the further issues of securities-market data and antitrust analysis, economic aspects of antitrust, public-choice aspects of antitrust, antitrust as a substitute for socialism, comparisons with antitrust in other countries, the private bar and antitrust policy, compensation and antitrust policy, and state antitrust activities. The conference participants were

William Adams, Private Attorney
Mahoney, Hadlow, and Adams

William F. Baxter, Professor of Law
Stanford University

Harlan M. Blake, Professor of Law
Columbia University

Yale Brozen, Professor of Economics
Graduate School of Business, University of Chicago

Terry Calvani, Professor of Law
Vanderbilt University

Robert Crawford, Professor of Economics
Brigham Young University

Kenneth W. Dam, Professor of Law
University of Chicago

Richard E. Day, Dean, School of Law
University of South Carolina

Donald Dewey, Professor of Economics
Columbia University

Ross D. Eckert, Visiting Professor
Claremont Men's College

Ernest Gellhorn, Professor of Law
University of Virginia

Victor Goldberg, Professor of Economics
University of California, Davis

Lino Graglia, Professor of Law
University of Texas

Edmund Kitch, Professor of Law
University of Chicago

Henry Manne, Professor of Law
University of Miami

Jesse Markham, Professor of Economics
Graduate School of Business, Harvard University

Thomas Morgan, Professor of Law
University of Illinois

Walter Oi, Professor of Economics
University of Rochester

Peggy Radin, Professor of Law
University of Southern California

Warren Schwartz, Professor of Law
Georgetown University

John J. Siegfried, Professor of Economics
Vanderbilt University

Robert D. Tollison, Professor of Economics
Virginia Polytechnic Institute and State University

Oliver E. Williamson, Professor of Economics
University of Pennsylvania

I am grateful to the conference participants for their help in the preparation of this volume, and I conclude with the hope that the analysis and issues raised here will stimulate further research on the role of antitrust in the economy.

Robert D. Tollison
Virginia Polytechnic Institute
and State University

**Principal Paper
by William Baxter**

1 The Political Economy of Antitrust

William F. Baxter

The Political Constituency for Antitrust

In a rash moment, and without giving any thought to the difficulties which would beset the project, I agreed to write a paper which would attempt to identify the political constituency for the passage and enforcement of the antitrust laws in the United States. As a first approximation, it may be supposed that this problem is the same as the question who actually wins and who actually loses from the enforcement of the antitrust laws. The conventional response to these questions, and the first hypothesis of the paper, is that public-spirited legislators pass these laws and the public-spirited judiciary enforces them because they benefit all consumers in that their effect is to improve resource allocation by minimizing the occurrence of the monopolistic prices which would otherwise be charged by single firm monopolists and by cartels.

I do not wish to dismiss casually the possibility that this conventional answer may be correct, in whole or in part. Yet obviously, to embark on the undertaking represented by this paper implies that the conventional answer is viewed with skepticism. Reasons tending to justify such skepticism come readily to mind. First, to say that a political constituency consists of everyone comes perilously close, because of obvious free-rider problems, to saying it consists of no one. The more sharply focused interests of potential monopolists and cartel members might be expected to cause them to be more effective politically, the susceptibility of these groups to free-rider problems being far less.

Second, although certain portions of the antitrust laws and their application seem, from a theoretical economic standpoint, to be quite consistent with the conventional response, other portions are much less so. In the first category, I would include application of Section 1 of the Sherman Act to horizontal collusion, application of Section 2 of the Sherman Act to various types of predatory behavior by firms with very large market shares, applications of Section 1 of the Sherman Act and Section 7 of the Clayton Act to horizontal mergers within concentrated markets, and applications of Section 8 of the Clayton Act to interlocking directorates between horizontal competitors in concentrated markets. Much less clearly justifiable are the theoretical underpinnings of most applications of the Sherman Act to vertical arrangements, of Section 3 of the Clayton Act, and of Sections 7 and 8

3

of the Clayton Act outside the contexts previously described. And it is barely conceivable that the Robinson-Patman Act might further efficient allocation.

Even if it is conceded that many applications of the antitrust laws, and indeed substantially all applications of some portions of them, tend to worsen rather than improve resource allocation, the conventional response need not necessarily be rejected. When the existence of such governmental malfunctions can no longer be denied, they are often accommodated by the observation that nobody is perfect. The legislation itself can be regarded as reflecting an intellectual failure by legislators in their economic analysis, or a failure by legislators to forecast accurately how judges and bureaucrats might mistakenly apply the laws they had written. The remedy, it follows, is the selection of "better" public servants.

The adequacy of these conventional responses becomes less and less tenable when confronted by the longevity and vitality of the supposed errors. Legislators persist in their intellectual lapses notwithstanding an endless series of patient, and often condescending, economic instruction. And administrators continue to be appointed who, in the face of similar lectures, either blunder in their application of the law or, in their interpretive processes, pursue some set of social objectives quite different from allocative efficiency.

For these reasons, the conventional view of the world is regarded with great skepticism by many social scientists—probably including most economists. In their view, although all of the people make mistakes some of the time and some of the people make mistakes all of the time, a persistent pattern of behavior which is exhibited by a large fraction of a population of significant size must be regarded as reflecting a preference held by the actors and cannot accurately be attributed to persistent error. The pattern is seen as strong evidence of revealed demand for the results which the behavioral pattern produces. The present paper is in this tradition: its underlying premise is that major subparts of the antitrust laws consistently produce results which are antithetical to the goal of economic efficiency; and it ascribes that outcome to a demand for those inefficient results by some group which holds political influence in the particular political context of antitrust.

If the inefficient aspects of antitrust are to be explained as the product of self-interested exertion of political influence, we must entertain some hypothesis as to the groups who perceive that they benefit from those inefficiencies and the avenues through which they exercise political influence. At various points in time over the years I have worked at antitrust, I have entertained several different hypotheses of this kind.

Perhaps the most obvious of these several hypotheses starts from the observation that the most direct beneficiary of much antitrust activity is the private antitrust bar. I explore this second hypothesis only briefly because it seems to me inconsistent with the very substantial evidence that can be gathered through casual empiricism. A brief statement of the facts to which I refer follows. First, at least until very recent years, the organized antitrust bar consisted almost entirely of a defendant's antitrust bar. Although the group did not benefit any the less because all of their activities were on behalf of defendants, their client relationships posed great obstacles to open political advocacy of stringent antitrust rules or antitrust enforcement. Second, over the past twenty years I have had sporadic contact with the antitrust section of the American Bar Association; and, although that group contains a sprinkling of members who are apologists for inefficient antitrust, usually on the ground that a certain amount of it is politically necessary in order to avoid more extensive government intervention through regulation, there is little question that the group as a whole is hostile to stringent antitrust rules and enforcement. The group as a whole seems to me surprisingly insensitive to the distinction between those portions of antitrust which are probably conducive to efficiency and those portions of antitrust which are almost certainly antithetical to efficiency; nevertheless their basic political position more nearly reflects the economic interests of their large corporate clients than it does their own interest as collectors of legal fees. Third, a point which will be documented hereafter, an examination of congressional hearings on antitrust over the years reveals few instances where active members of the antitrust bar have urged the passage of inefficient antitrust rules.

A third hypotheses I have entertained from time to time is arguably merely a modified version of the conventional view as it depends upon the premise of long-lived misperception by the voting public. Yet there is an important difference between the conventional view and the present hypothesis in that not everyone is mistaken in the context of the present hypothesis. The hypothesis is that there are no private interests which form an effective constituency for antitrust; the constituency consists of public officials who view antitrust as a relatively low cost vehicle for the expansion of their own power and their own budgets. It is low cost because, just as there is no politically effective private interest constituency for antitrust, so also there is no politically effective constituency against it. Political costs which may be incurred as a result of opposition by foreseeable corporate defendants are at least partially offset by the ability of elected official proponents to play upon widespread populist attitudes among the voting public. The validity of this view does not rest on an assumption that the vote-gathering potential of this populist posturing is high, provided that the number of votes lost is low. I would expect that the electoral gains are not high; for the number of voters able to identify their representative's attitudes on antitrust must be very small, and the number who can distinguish between efficient antitrust rules and inefficient rules must be vanishingly small. Even in the case of the very small number of voters who have perceptions on these matters, the frequency with which antitrust policy is regarded as an issue of political saliency that would cause such an individual to vote for or against a representative must also be very low. Hence this hypothesis depends only on the requirement that the direct losers, probably defendants, are unable to impose sufficient direct political costs to offset the sum of direct political gains through populist posturing and indirect gains in the form of public-sector expansion.

There is a sense in which this third hypothesis, like the conventional view, depends upon the premise of long-lived misperception on the part of voters. But it differs from the conventional view in at least one, and arguably two, respects. First there is a set of gainers, public officials, who are not persistently mistaken.

The second difference to which I refer is not so much a factual difference as it is a disposition on my part to disagree with the behavioralist proposition that substantial populations do not persist in a mistaken perception of their own self-interest over significant time horizons. I have no doubt that when individuals repeatedly engage in relatively simple financial transactions, a learning process occurs very rapidly. If a product which is advertised to be canned chicken soup in fact contains no chicken, consumers may be fooled into buying one can or perhaps three; but their willingness to pay more than the price charged for whatever substance the cans do contain will disappear very quickly. And so long as attention is confined to choices whose results follow more or less contemporaneously with the exercise of choice, there is considerable evidence that accurate intuitive perceptions will be developed even when intellectual comprehension is thwarted by the complexity of the transactions. Thus in an environment where interest payments on demand deposits are prohibited by Regulation Q, people maintain greater balances when market interest rates are low than when they are high; and in their use of credit cards, the extent to which different income groups take advantage of the opportunity to pay less than all of their current charges and to permit their balances to "revolve" at an interest cost approaching 20 percent per annum on a compound basis appears to be closely related to the typical capital costs each of those groups faces in capital markets.

But even in the realm of individual financial transactions, as transactions become increasingly complex, as the frequency with which the transaction is performed lessens, and as the results of choice are separated temporally from the exercise of choice, the tendency for systematic error to disappear appears to be greatly attenuated. For example, there appears to be enormous disparity in internal rates of return among various, widely sold, whole life insurance policies.

When attention is shifted from individual financial choices to individual voting behavior, it seems to me doubtful that one should expect results, even over very substantial periods, to reveal preferences actually held by the voting population, at least with respect to any political issues except that very small number of issues which dominates public attention. Political markets are characterized by all the problems of those economic markets where learning seems to proceed most slowly. First, the complexity problem alone is often great. Second, the range of policy choice is obscure, for the position of a candidate on many issues will not be known; and the results of the particular choice can be known, if at all, only after many years have passed. Third, the results of choice are never perceived by the individual in a way that he is able to associate with the choice he made; and the magnitude with which the results affect the individual are relatively small. But in addition to, and quite independent of, all these informational difficulties, there is the problem of issues saliency—only rarely does the individual voter have an opportunity to choose between candidates on the basis of their positions on antitrust generally, still less on their positions toward inefficient antitrust. Even if that opportunity were afforded more frequently than it is, the opportunity would be declined in a great preponderance of cases, for other differences between the candidates would be more important to most individual voters.

One cannot escape from this incomparability between economic and voting choices by pointing out that entry is relatively easy into the political arena and that a new aspiring candidate is free to base his campaign on any group of issues he chooses. These factors create at most an illusion that there is room for endless product variation in electoral markets; for they pertain to primary campaigns, not to final runoffs, and then only to a limited degree. The candidate's costs of communicating his positions on various issues is a positive function of the number of issues he wishes to address. If there are three or four or five issues about which a substantial majority of the population cares most, and if antitrust policy is not among these, as it surely will not be, then rarely if ever will it be cost effective for a candidate to attempt to differentiate himself with respect to his position on antitrust policy; and the frequency with which circumstances conducive to differentiation will arise will decrease as the number of serious candidates decreases.

The problem is akin to that pointed out by Steiner years ago in the context of "free" radio broadcasting. If the audience for type A program material is five times the size of the audience which prefers type B, then the first five stations in a market all will have an incentive to broadcast type A and capture their expected share of the substantial majority; unless there are six or more stations, no one will broadcast type B. In political markets it is highly atypical for the number of broadcasters to exceed two.

Of course these observations may cease to hold if, within the candidate's constituency, there is a private interest group which may experience substantial gains or losses as a consequence of the candidate's position on the nonsalient issue. That private group may then respond with campaign assistance, thus revealing their intensity of preference with respect to that issue. But if no such private interest exists, and my hypothesis is that none does, then the broadcasting analogy applies. Candidates will be elected without reference to their position on antitrust policy, and their preference for an antitrust policy which expands the public sector without regard for its efficiency consequences can be costlessly indulged.

The fourth and last hypothesis which has from time to time appealed to me as plausible is that the continuing struggle over antitrust policy is most accurately perceived as a struggle between large and smaller business enterprises. This hypothesis is particularly appealing because it would predict the emergence not merely of a large and activist antitrust apparatus but of a designedly inefficient antitrust apparatus to the extent that the latter group succeeded through the political arena, in imposing cost handicaps on the former.

The image implicit in this hypothesis, that of a world of commerce divided categorically into a group of large firms and a discrete group of small firms, is obviously unrealistic. Data on business demographics suggests that size distribution is continuous in most industries, with the number of firms at each size category decreasing as the size of the firms within the category increases. And obviously, there is great variance from one industry to the next in the absolute size of a firm that would be regarded as being of middle size in its industry. But simplification is necessary to facilitate preliminary empiric testing of the hypothesis, and the simplification need not impair the explanatory power of even this crude model if it is roughly true that within many industries there is a group of firms which perceive themselves to be small within the industry, and they are successfully using the political process to advance their interests in their rivalry with firms in the industry perceived to be large.

Another doubt that one must entertain about this model is its implication that, in many industries, small firms are, or perceive themselves to be, in competition with large firms to a high degree, but to be in competition with other small firms only to a lesser degree. At first glance, that seems most unlikely to be true; yet we cannot permit the hypothesis to be amended so that it rests merely on the perception by small firms that the proposition is true (although it is false) for then we would have returned to the behavioralistically unacceptable stance of entertaining a hypothesis that rests on an enduring mistake.

Yet unless the proposition is true, no substantial advantage can be obtained by the small firms in an industry by handicapping the large firms; for any monopolistic rents that might be available immediately after any given legal change would quickly be bid away by rivalry among the small firms.

Hence if the hypothesis is to be saved, we must go on to postulate some sense in which it is true that large firms represent a competitive threat to small firms in a sense that other small firms do not. If it is assumed that both large firms and other small firms compete with small firms along all of the same parameters of price, physical quality, completeness of inventory, service and convenience at the point of sale, and so forth, then I believe it would be impossible to frame a tenable theory by which small firms could gain by handicapping larger ones, but if the competition between the sets is of a different character than the competition among the small set of firms, then perhaps the hypothesis may be saved.

I find the following model a plausible one. The firm occupies a point in space. Because in every industry there are economies of scale to some degree (if there were none, the ultimate consumer would perform the function for himself and there would be no industry), every firm can be viewed as being a natural monopoly with respect to some geographical enclave surrounding its location. Whether this enclave is substantial or trivial depends on just how extensive the scale economies are, on the density distribution of customers across the firm's and adjoining enclaves, and on transport costs. That natural monopoly phenomenon exists both because the firm's own cost curves are negatively sloped over some output range and because there is a positive cost to customers in traveling to the firm's point in space and transporting the good or service back to its ultimate point of consumption. Thus the nearby customer's cost saving, deriving from propinquity to the firm, creates an appropriatable surplus. What constrains the maximum price that can be charged by the small firm is the customer's cost of traveling to and from the next most proximate firm and the price that is being charged by the next most proximate firm; and travel cost will be greater as scale economies are greater, inducing wider spacing of firms. (In this paragraph I speak as if the costs of conquering space were always borne directly by the consumer; actually it is irrelevant whether the consumer or the firm itself does the transporting.) Given any particular state of technology, this model yields a more or less stable equilibrium of firms distributed over space. (Employment of discriminatory prices may also be a necessary condition for stable equilibrium.)

But two different types of technological change can upset this equilibrium. First, if the costs of overcoming space are reduced, and thus the advantage of propinquity lessened, theretofore unexploited economies of scale can be realized; firms will grow larger, moving down their negatively sloped cost curves, and a new equilibrium will emerge which involves fewer, larger firms, less densely distributed over space.

2. Second, technology may affect production functions; and all relevant

changes reduce the absolute level of the production function at at least one point along its output range. Obviously not every such change can also be characterized as increasing economies of scale. Yet it seems plausible to assume that many if not most do have that effect.

Any occurrence of the first type of technological change and any occurrence of a scale increasing technological change of the second type will tend toward the displacement of many smaller firms by fewer larger ones.

The period of history spanned by the antitrust laws is one in which very dramatic technological change of the first kind has occurred. Obviously all improvements in transportation fall in that category as do many improvements in communications. Technological changes affecting the production function probably have been no less rapid; for the most part they have been too heterogeneous to mention. But one particular change, scale economies in advertising attributable to radio, to television, and to the fact that daily newspapers have rapidly declined in number and expanded in average geographic coverage, undoubtedly has had a major impact on many industries. The scale effect here derives in large part from the comparative inefficiency of advertising by a firm which is not represented ubiquitously throughout the smallest geographic area which can be reached at minimum cost by these broadside media.

Another technological change likely to have been of very widespread impact is that of communications and data-processing technology on the span of management control. These permit the cost of highly specialized and highly expert management to be spread over geographically dispersed branch, or franchised, outlets, each of which individually enjoys propinquity with respect to a given customer set.

Tending in the opposite direction, that is toward the multiplication of small firms, or at least of local outlets, and yielding increases in the value of propinquity, is the marked increase in the time costs of many consumers. The enormous success of the 7-Eleven grocery chain is probably a manifestation of that factor. But, as the example illustrates, that factor is conducive as much to the multiplication of outlets of large establishments as it is to the multiplication of enterprises. Hence, on balance it is quite plausible to assume that the historic period of antitrust has confronted the small enterprise almost continuously with the threat of, and often the fact of, displacement by larger enterprises. This threat might correctly be perceived as posing dangers of quite different magnitude from those posed by price competition from the next most proximate shopkeeper down the road and from the appearance of a new shopkeeper just around the block.

This fourth and last hypothesis, then, restated with reference to the refinements developed in the preceding paragraphs, is that small business, usually making its political weight felt through the trade association, has effectively employed the antitrust laws to retard but not halt the continuous encroachment on its territorial enclaves by larger enterprises using superior production technologies and often achieving the attribute of propinquity through networks of branch outlets.

Data by which the Alternative Hypotheses Can Be Tested

In this part of the paper I discuss data sets which are available, or which might be constructed, with which some progress might be made in testing the several hypotheses set forth previously.

Antitrust Litigation

To most lawyers, antitrust litigation would appear to be the most obvious body of evidence to which to turn in any investigation of the purposes or effects of the antitrust laws. Perhaps that professional predisposition would be sound if we actually had available any objective measures of the population of antitrust controversies. But we do not. Even if one were to undertake the monumental task of examining the records of individual federal district courts back over the years, the investigator would find himself examining only a small sample of antitrust controversies; and there is little assurance that the sample would be random with respect to any characteristic of interest.

I know of no way of ascertaining the percentage of antitrust controversies which survived the process of initial negotiation and investigation and resulted in the filing of either a public or a private suit. Survey data in other areas of legal controversy indicate that the percentage of claims filed in those areas is quite small. But the basic problem is not one of sample size; it is that very little if anything can reliably be inferred about the population from the sample. It is highly probable that filed cases constitute a sample that is biased in several respects—they are likely to consist disproportionately of controversies in which the stakes are relatively high and in which the parties diverge in their estimations of the outcome of pursuing the matter further.

Although I would be prepared to argue that this proposition holds as well for actions commenced by government as for private actions, the basic point can be made most simply in the context of the private action. Because the line of analysis has been developed at considerable length in other papers and probably is familiar to most readers, I will not pursue it at great length nor with all the refinements that other writers have brought to bear upon it. I believe that the model I developed and presented to my faculty colleagues ten years ago has the advantages both of simplicity and clarity in revealing the core of the problem.

It is assumed that neither party faces operable capital constraints and that each is risk neutral. (Risk neutrality is assumed merely for convenience. Relaxation of the assumption with regard to either or both parties yields a higher proportion of settlements.) The plaintiff assigns some probability to his winning should the case go to litigation and predicts that he will be awarded some specific sum of damages if he wins. Litigation will involve expense to him; and his present expected value of pursuing litigation is the product of his probability figure times his damage figure less his litigation expenses. The situation from the defendant's standpoint is analogous. He may assess the probabilities of plaintiff's victory differently than does the plaintiff and may predict a different magnitude of damage award; but he too will have expenses. His expected present costs if the controversy goes to litigation is his probability figure times his damage figure plus his litigation expenses. If both parties behave rationally in their own financial interest, the case will be settled rather than litigated if the sum of their litigation expenses exceeds the disparity between their probabilistic estimates of outcome; for under these circumstances there are gains from trade to be had by settlement.

Let the variables P, D, and E represent, respectively, the probability of a plaintiff judgment, the magnitude of the damage award, and expense of litigation; and let the subscripts p and d indicate the person who is assigning an expected value to the associated variable. Then the case is likely to be litigated only if

$$(P_d D_d) + E_d < (P_p D_p) - E_p; \text{ or} \tag{1.1}$$

$$[E_d + E_p] + (P_d D_d) - (P_p D_p) < 0. \tag{1.2}$$

In general, then, the settlement range can be described graphically as follows:

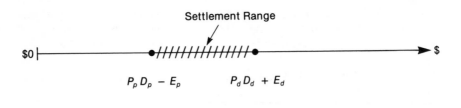

Settlement Range

$P_p D_p - E_p$ $P_d D_d + E_d$

No Settlement Possible

$P_d D_d + E_d$ $P_p D_p - E_p$

Thus it is clear that a case is likely to be settled if $(P_d D_d)$ is equal or nearly equal to $(P_p D_p)$. A case will be litigated when the disparity between those two products exceeds the sum of the parties' costs of litigating. Since the costs of litigation are always positive, and in many antitrust cases are enormous, litigation will occur only when the expectations that the parties hold about the probability of outcome or about the magnitude of the award, or both, differ substantially.

Hence, while the existence of controversies is a necessary condition, it is by no means a sufficient condition for litigation; substantial uncertainty as to outcome is also necessary.

The uncertainty which will lead to the necessary disparity in expectations may arise from several sources: uncertainty as to what the facts will be found to be by the trier of fact, uncertainty as to the amount of harm which the plaintiff will be found to have suffered, and uncertainty as to the substance of rules of law which will be applied and how they will be applied to the facts as found.

As the work of others has shown, it is clear that these are not the only variables that might sensibly be included in a model of litigation. For example, one can disaggregate D_d, as Landes and Posner[1] did in their paper, so as to model the circumstance of parties who have a continuing stake in the doctrinal content of the law in addition to having an expectation at some probability level that he will be required to pay damages in the instant case. Although I have no theoretical difficulty with such attempted refinement, neither the variables I have included nor those I find in the models of others are composed of factors likely to shed light on the question who systematically wins or loses as a consequence of antitrust enforcement.

Some interesting implications about litigated cases can be drawn from the very simple model I have proposed. First, if the appraisals of P and D by the parties are roughly equal, the case will not be litigated; the second two terms of 1.2 negate one another, and the potential gains from settlement correspond to the aggregate costs of litigation.

Second, if the parties' estimations of the magnitude of D are roughly equal to one another, then litigation will occur only if their respective estimations of P diverge substantially and diverge in a particular direction: P_p must exceed P_d. Divergence in the opposite direction has the effect of enlarging the settlement range. The magnitude of the sum of the last two terms approaches a maximum when P_p approaches one and P_d approaches zero. At this theoretical maximum, the case will be litigated if D_p exceeds the aggregate litigation costs. If the parties' estimations of P diverge less widely, then the magnitude of the consistently estimated D must increase geometrically if litigation is to result, and must increase without limit as the individual estimates of P approach equality.

Symmetrically, if the party's individual estimates of P are roughly equal, then their estimates of D_p and D_d must diverge substantially if litigation is to occur. And once again the plaintiff must be more optimistic than the defendant is pessimistic; divergence in the opposite direction produces settlement.

The circumstance most conducive to litigation is that in which both P_p and D_p exceed P_d and D_d, an event which might be expected to occur in only 25 percent of controversies if objective evaluations are being made. And even within this subset of cases, settlement will occur if aggregate litigation expenses exceed the resultant disparity. Since litigation expenses, even in relatively simple antitrust cases, are relatively high, we should not expect any significant amount of litigation where the stakes are relatively small and should expect a large fraction of all controversies to be settled.

It seems likely that the magnitude of litigation expense is not independent of the absolute size of D. It seems intuitively probable, an intuition that is confirmed by my own episodic involvement with antitrust litigation, that E, viewed as a function of D, is a positively sloped, downwardly concave function which has a substantial positive intercept and which may or may not approach an asymptote at very large values of D. If this is correct, then, relative to a world in which litigation costs could be treated as a constant, our ability to predict that small cases will be settled while large ones will be litigated is weakened: although it is true that, as the magnitude of the stakes (D) increase, ever smaller percentage differences in the parties' estimation of D and P will create a divergence of increasing absolute size thus tending toward litigation, the absolute magnitude of litigation expenses will also be increasing, tending towards settlement.

A final complication is that, although a mutual decision to settle will usually represent a once-and-for-all decision, a decision to litigate is of a quite different character. For litigation does not occur at a point in time but consists of a long series of events, often drawn out over substantial periods of time, which can be described in procedural terms. The passage of time and the serial occurrence of these events affect all the different variables in the algebraic model. I believe that the effects of the litigation process can be seen most clearly if we now permit the model to become slightly more complicated. We take account of the fact that P_p and P_d are not probabilistic estimates of the outcome of a single event but rather that each represents a compounded probability estimate based on probabilistic estimations of outcomes of each of the series of procedural events that constitutes litigation.

To illustrate. Today we were unable to reach a settlement agreement. Tomorrow the court will rule whether a class will be certified under Rule 23; if so, it would rule shortly thereafter on how notice to the class is to be given. Months later it will rule whether a given group of documents is privileged or subject to discovery; later still on how the factual inquiry at trial is to be bounded by the running of the four year statute of limitations. Over time, discovery will occur; and this may go well or badly. A jury will be empaneled, the composition of which may be favorable or unfavorable but will not be known until that time. At trial there will be more procedural rulings on admissibility; moreover our opponents may or may not have the insight—or will it be luck—to call nonobvious witness Mr. W., whose testimony, if he is forced to testify, will hurt us badly.

On each of these events counsel for each of the parties has, implicitly or explicitly, placed a probability number that the outcome will be favorable to plaintiff. The variable P which appears in the model is a mathematical compound of these often independent but sometimes interdependent probabilities. As the litigation proceeds and each of these events passes from expectation to history, its probability assessment takes on a value of one or zero; and at each stage the residual, now somewhat less compound, probability assessment attached to all those events which are yet to come must be recalculated. With each recalculation, P jumps up toward one or down toward zero as the good news or bad news rolls in. The parties' expectations as to the correct value to assign to D will be bounced about in similar fashion by some but not all of these procedural events.

It will generally be clear enough after the occurrence of any procedural event for whom it was bad news. Consequently the values of the residuals P_p and P_d will generally shift in the same direction, although probably not by the same magnitude, on the occurrence of each event. These differences in the magnitude of shifts, notwithstanding that they are in the same direction and therefore to a degree offsetting, may themselves result today in the settlement of a case which could not have been settled yesterday.

But two other changes are continuously occurring during litigation in the values assigned to variables in the model. First, and most obviously, as the case progresses, litigation expenses that once might have been avoided by settlement are converted to sunk costs. The consequence of this change is continuously to narrow the settlement range and make settlement less likely.

On the other hand, the number of procedural events with unknown outcomes is reduced with the passage of time. Intuitively, and again partially as a result of personal experience, it seems clear that the general tendency of this reduction is to cause the values respectively assigned to P_p and P_d to converge, although not necessarily monotonically.

This tendency toward convergence, conducive to settlement, tends to offset the consequences of the fact that litigation expenses are continuously converted to sunk costs. At any stage of the trial either tendency may be occurring with greater pace than the other. Hence at any moment the parties may find themselves further than ever from a settlement agreement or, alternatively, a case previously not susceptible to settlement may settle readily at a given procedural stage.

The implications of this model may be summarized as follows. Because each party is advised by a professional, the actual but undisclosed value assignments by each party to the variables P and D will, more often than not, be commensurate. A substantial amount of bluffing by each party about the values he has assigned to the variables is to be expected; controversies will not be settled easily or quickly. But as expenses are incurred and even greater expenses become imminent, the parties are driven toward more honest disclosures of their appraisals, and most cases are settled. As the procedural steps of litigation unfold, still additional cases are settled and litigation abandoned.

Of the cases that are litigated all the way to some final judgment, one's initial expectation might be that plaintiffs and defendants should each win a roughly equal proportion; for there is no reason to think that the cases in which a skillful and objective value assignment to P is greater (or less) than .5 are more likely to be litigated than those in which P is less (or greater) than .5. It is disparity between the party's estimates that leads to litigation, and this disparity can occur as well at high absolute values as at low values. But as previously noted, absolutely large values of D are conducive to litigation.

Although I would expect this model to hold well for many types of private litigation, it does not appear to hold at all well with respect to private antitrust litigation. In table 1-1, data are presented regarding the disposition of private antitrust cases for the years 1964–1970.

Observe that although the number of cases decided over these years varies significantly from year to year, the percentage which appears in any given row over the years is somewhat more stable. The figure in the last column is the weighted arithmetic mean of the numbers in the first seven columns of that row. These data are consistent with implications of the model in one important respect. Quite apart from the number of controversies which are settled prior to a filing of any complaint, the great preponderance of cases which proceeded as far as the preliminary stages of litigation, about 80 percent, appear to have been resolved by settlement between the parties.

On the other hand, the data are remarkably inconsistent with the implications of the model in another respect. Of the approximately 15 percent of cases that were resolved by judgment for one party or the other, defendants won judgments in about 85 percent.

I am unable to postulate any satisfactory hypothesis which makes this striking result harmonize with the simple model I have proposed. The most obvious, but not a very satisfactory, reconciliation is to suppose that plaintiffs are systematically and substantially overoptimistic about their prospects for success. Because plaintiff's overoptimism is bounded as the "objective" value of P approaches one, and because in cases where the

Table 1-1
Disposition of Private Antitrust Cases: 1964-1970

	1964	1965	1966	1967	1968	1969	1970	Seven-Year Average
Number of cases	749	1025	1141	436	402	443	505	671
Percentage of cases by disposition:								
Default judgment	0.0	0.0	0.0	0.2	0.2	0.0	0.0	0.0
Consent judgment	1.2	0.3	0.4	0.9	1.2	1.1	3.6	1.0
Dismissed: want of prosecution	2.0	2.0	1.0	2.3	3.5	4.1	2.8	2.2
Dismissed: action of parties	74.2	88.9	89.3	78.0	75.6	78.1	72.4	81.7
Judgment for plaintiff	1.1	1.6	1.5	3.0	2.7	3.8	4.8	2.3
Judgment for defendant	21.5	7.2	7.9	15.6	16.7	12.9	16.4	12.8
Percentage of litigated won by plaintiff	4.9	18.2	16.0	16.1	13.9	23.0	22.6	15.2

Source: Part of the underlying data are taken from Posner, "A Statistical Study of Antitrust Enforcement," 13 *Journal of Law and Economics,* p. 383, Table 13; the rest was obtained from the Administrative Office of the U.S. courts. This table differs from Posner's Table 13 in that I have omitted cases in which no judgment was entered, cases remanded to state courts, cases transferred to other federal courts, and one miscellaneous case in each 1964 and 1968 and have converted the numerical instances into percentages of the column total in rows below the first row.

objective value of P is large, the more realistic defendants will make generous offers resulting in settlement, the remaining cases pushed through the litigation process are disproportionately those in which plaintiff's chances, "objectively" evaluated, are very poor.

Again in this context I am disposed to reject this hypothesis because it rests on a premise involving systematic error by a class of persons, each acting in the context of his own financial affairs. But one possible reconciliation is to suppose that although antitrust defendants are well and faithfully represented by their counsel, antitrust plaintiffs typically fall into the clutches of lawyers who are more interested in collecting litigation fees than in advancing the interests of their clients. If antitrust defendants typically are larger corporations with established relationships with outside law firms that value the long term client relationship more highly than the short term capture of litigation fees, whereas antitrust plaintiffs are typically smaller firms without such law firm relationships and typically are represented by lawyers who have no prospect for a continuing relationship and hence maximize in the short run by dishonest representations about the prospects for litigation success, this reconciliation can be made plausible. Although that set of relationships no doubt exists in some cases, it seems to me unlikely to be typical.

An alternative harmonizing assumption is that the initial probability distribution of P is highly skewed toward $P = 1$ (that is, $\overline{P} < .5$), and that this characteristic is incompletely filtered out by the settlement process. This is possible if a large fraction of antitrust claims are meritless strike suits in which plaintiffs are attempting to shake defendants down for a fraction of their expected litigation expenses, E_d, and if defendants respond, at least in some instances, to the long run incentive to deter such conduct rather than accepting the shakedown. But any particular defendant pays all the costs of deterrence and receives only a fraction of the benefits. This, too, seems unlikely to explain the observed value of P in litigated cases.

I think that more promising results can be obtained if the model, insofar as it depicts a negotiating posture of the antitrust defendant, is amended. In a large fraction of antitrust cases, the defendant's business relationship to the plaintiff is not the only relationship of that type which he enjoys. If the plaintiff is a customer, there are many other customers who might raise substantially the same complaint. If plaintiff is a supplier or a competitor, there are likely to be other suppliers or competitors with similar potential complaints. Hence, in the process of negotiating settlement, the defendant must take into account that, if he makes any substantial settlement payment to the plaintiff, he will whet the appetite of analogously related potential claimants. Hence I introduce a new variable, B, which represents a magnitude of the burden the defendant will bear in dealing with other parties as a consequence of agreeing to any nontrivial settlement in plaintiff's favor.

On the other hand, if there are other parties waiting in the wings as we have supposed, the defendant will make matters worse rather than better if he litigates the case and loses. If he settles, he probably can get the plaintiff to agree to maintain silence about the fact and magnitude of the settlement and perhaps to return or to destroy damaging documents which plaintiff has in his possession. But if defendant litigates unsuccessfully, his vulnerability to the claims of others will become publicized, and those damaging documents and perhaps others not yet discovered by plaintiff will pass into the public domain. Hence his loss function in the event of unsuccessful litigation must include some multiple of B, MB, where $M > 1$. If on the other hand he litigates successfully, the analogously situated parties are likely to be effectively deterred from pressing similar claims. His loss in this event consists of his litigation costs; B is avoided.

I rewrite the model with these modifications. From the plaintiff's standpoint, the value of pressing forward through litigation is, as before, $P_p D_p - E_p$. Plaintiff is willing to settle if the settlement offer is of that magnitude or greater.

From defendant's perspective the costs of going on through litigation will be expressed as the arithmetic sum of four terms. The first, as before, is $(P_d D_d)$. The second term is $(P_d MB)$, the plaintiff's chances of success as evaluated by defendant multiplied times the enlarged burden defendant will bear in dealing with other parties. This term encourages settlement and discourages litigation. The third term is E_d, as before, defendant's litigation expenses. The fourth term, carrying a negative sign, is B—the burden which he will bear in dealing with other parties as a consequence of settlement, a term which deters settlement and encourages litigation. It can be avoided only by successful litigation.

Viewing the matter in this light, the case will be settled if:

$$P_p D_p - E_p < P_d (D_d + MB) - B + E_d;$$

or equivalently:

$$[E_d + E_p] + B[P_d M - 1] > P_p D_p - P_d D_d;$$

otherwise it will be litigated.

If we now make the further assumption that the parties, or their counsel, will make skillful and objective evaluations of the magnitudes D_p, D_d, P_p and P_d and that those appraisals will be roughly equal, we can substitute the common estimates, P and D, and rewrite the conditions for settlement as follows:

$$[E_d + E_p] + B[PM - 1] > P(D_p - D_d);$$

$$[E_d + E_p] + B[PM - 1] > 0.$$

This last algebraic expression of the model is susceptible to an appealing interpretation which is also consistent with the data in table 1–1. It is appealing, first, because it indicates that a particular subset of cases will be litigated even when both D_p and D_d and P_p and P_d are roughly equal; hence we need no longer assume enduring systematic error in the appraisals of plaintiffs in order to explain the observed results.

As before, the aggregate of litigation expenses continue to operate as a force for settlement. Also as before, any amount by which D_p exceeds D_d continues to operate as a force for litigation. Whether the disparity in damage estimates is a strong or weak force for litigation depends on both the absolute magnitude of the disparity and the common perception of the parties as to the strength of plaintiff's case. The significance of the damage disparity as a force for litigation diminishes as the parties mutually estimate the plaintiff's chances of success to be small; for as P moves from one towards zero, the aggregate of litigation expenses is evermore likely to exceed the disparity in expected outcomes.

The more interesting feature of the model is the second term to the left of the inequality. B, the burden with respect to other parties that defendant must bear as a result of settlement, is always positive. But the second factor in that term need not be positive; although it is assumed the M always equals or exceeds one, P is always less than one; and if the product, (PM), is less than one, then the entire second term becomes negative and becomes a force for litigation. Hence the weaker plaintiff's case, as commonly evaluated by the parties, is perceived to be, given any constant value for M, the stronger is the defendant's incentive to litigate in order to deter similarly situated parties. As plaintiff's case grows stronger, however, the second left-hand term becomes an additional force for settlement. Defendant's incentive to litigate becomes a negative function of P.

The data in table 1–1 indicate that in those private antitrust cases which are actually litigated, the average value of P is about .15. It follows that the second term becomes insignificant when the value of M is about 7, the reciprocal of .15. If we can assume that M holds the value of about 7 in the typical antitrust case, then the lightning rod phenomenon represented by B becomes a force for settlement when P takes on values greater than .15 and a force for litigation for values of P less than .15. Since the data suggest that the average value for P across litigated cases is about .15, it seems plausible to assume that P is uniformly distributed around $P = .15$, that antitrust cases are likely to be litigated when P ranges from .3 to something approaching zero and that the value of M ranges upward from 3 across the set of litigated cases.

Although this model of the antitrust settlement-negotiation process makes more sense of the data than any other I have been able to devise, it gives us very little assistance in using litigated antitrust cases to answer our central question, who wins and who loses. For although we can infer that antitrust victims, and hence successful antitrust plaintiffs, are likely to be members of a class each of whom has been treated similarly by the defendant, the model gives us no insight into the characteristics of that class. It is equally consistent to suggest that the plaintiff and the third persons waiting in the wings are customers who have been charged cartel prices, to suggest alternatively that they are competitors seeking to deter the use of some superior technology available to the defendant, or to suggest that they are customers who, having negotiated a set of contracts with the defendant are now seeking to employ some inefficient antitrust rule to achieve judicial amendment to those contracts so as to redistribute rents in their favor. In order to employ antitrust cases for the purpose of shedding light on this basic inquiry, one would have to know more than I have been able to find out about the character of the claims made, not just in the 15 percent of filed cases that are eventually litigated, but in the 85 percent of the filed cases that are settled prior to final judgment and in the unknown number of controversies never filed but negotiated and settled at nontrivial payoffs to plaintiffs. The litigated cases are known to be a nonrandom sample of cases filed with respect to P, and there seems to me to be no persuasive reason to assume that the litigated subset is not nonrandom with respect to the character of the other controversies, either because the character of the complaints is correlated with the value of P or for some other reason.

Because the model just described did not prove to be useful with respect to the central question, I have not made any serious attempt to test it empirically; but one possible empiric test comes readily to mind. The model differs from the simpler model previously described primarily in the role played by the variables B and M. These variables appear in the model because it is assumed that a very large fraction of antitrust cases are potentially class action cases that are filed in a form that invokes far fewer plaintiffs than constitute the most encompassing possible class. If this is accurate, the significance of the role played by B and M should have been larger before than after the adoption in 1966 of major amendments to Rule 23 of the federal rules. It may also be true that the significance of B and M were smaller before than after Supreme Court's 1974 decision in the *Eisen* case. If those relationships hold, the percentage of filed claims litigated should have fallen and the percentage of plaintiff victories in cases litigated to judgment should have increased when Rule 23 was amended; and then both percentages should have shifted in the opposite direction after the decision in *Eisen*.

Unfortunately the Administrative Office of the Federal Courts collected data on antitrust case dispositions only during the period 1964–1970, so no data readily available permit testing for the effect of *Eisen*. But the data do embrace 1966, the date of amendment to Rule 23. In table 1–2 the rows correspond to those in table 1–1 but the columns have been aggregated into pre- and postamendment periods. The apparent discontinuities in the rows after 1966 all tend to support the implications of the model; the percentage of cases settled drops, the percentage of substantially all types of alternative outcomes rises, and the percentage of cases litigated to final judgment won by plaintiffs rises. The mean value of P in fully litigated cases appears to rise from about 11 percent to about 19 percent.

Even an examination of complaints filed may prove to be less informative than might be hoped. One of the interesting implications of the model is that a plaintiff with a reasonably good case could increase his probable settlement recovery by conducting himself so as to maximize the value of M, thus maximizing the difference in the defendant's burden toward third parties under conditions of complete litigation as compared with conditions of settlement. Perhaps the most obvious way to accomplish this result is for plaintiff to approach defendant privately, not filing any complaint at all. But if plaintiff finds it necessary to file a complaint in order to get defendant's serious attention, he would do well to file a complaint that is as vague as possible and tends to conceal precisely those factors which rendered the defendant vulnerable to third parties. Hence, if the model is sound, filed complaints may reveal less about the true nature of the controversy than would be true in different contexts.

Such light as can be drawn from the implications of the model bearing on the central question is supportive, although only weakly so, of the "small-business" hypothesis. The model implies that antitrust defendants typically have a multiplicity of business relationships analogous to their relationship with the plaintiff. Because the role of the ultimate consumer as an antitrust plaintiff is of very recent vintage, this implies that the defendant has a multiplicity of analogous relationships with other businesses, and thus is unlikely itself to be a small enterprise. The model is consistent with the possibility that the plaintiff is either a large or a small enterprise. The implication that antitrust suits are typically brought by smaller enterprises against larger ones can be drawn only tenuously.

It may be true that all the light that can be shed by antitrust litigation on the several hypotheses framed at the beginning of this paper must be drawn, not from any microdata about the cases, but entirely from their aggregate numbers. In table 1–3 are displayed historic data about the aggregate number of antitrust cases decided in each five-year period from 1890 through 1975. In column 2 there appears the U.S. Gross National Product for each five-year period (expressed for all periods in 1958 dollars). Columns 3, 4, and 5 report Department of Justice cases won, lost, and total. In column 6, I have constructed an index of Department of Justice antitrust activity by dividing total DOJ cases for a period by the GNP level for the period and then adding enough zeros to produce a readable integer. The absolute size of these integers has no signficance; significance, if any, is to be found in the way the index rises and falls with the passage of time. Columns 7, 8, 9, and 10 present the same data for Federal Trade Commission activity. Columns 11 and 12 present the total number of private antitrust cases reported and an analogous activity index for private cases. Although data presented in table 1–3 are by five-year periods, I calculated the data on an annual basis; and in figure 1–1 I have plotted the index numbers on an annual basis.

The results are at least as puzzling as they are helpful. Department of Justice activity started at what, in retrospect, is a very low level; and then it fell further until 1905. Department of Justice activities shot upward rapidly from 1905 through 1914, the period which encompassed the Standard Oil

Table 1–2
Disposition of Private Antitrust Cases

	1964–1966	1967–1970
Number of cases	2915	1786
Percentage of cases by disposition:		
Default judgment	0.0	0.0
Consent judgment	0.6	1.8
Dismissed: want of prosecution	1.6	3.2
Dismissed: action of parties	85.3	75.9
Judgment for plaintiff	1.4	3.6
Judgment for defendant	11.1	15.4
Percent of litigated cases won by plaintiff	11.2	18.9

Source: Part of the underlying data are taken from Posner, "A Statistical Study of Antitrust Enforcement," 13 *Journal of Law and Economics,* p. 383, Table 13; the rest was obtained from Administrative Office of the U.S. courts. This table differs from Posner's Table 13 in that I have omitted cases in which no judgment was entered, cases remanded to state courts, cases transferred to other federal courts, and one miscellaneous case in each 1964 and 1968 and have converted the numerical instances into percentages of the column total in rows below the first row.

and Tobacco cases. If it is correct to assume that reported cases lag behind by several years the policy changes which result in their commencement, this historical high in the index perhaps should be attributed to the trust-busting enthusiasm of the Teddy Roosevelt administration. And perhaps the rapid decline thereafter must be attributed to the popular understanding of the implications of the Rule of Reason pronouncements, although objectively it is difficult to see why that pronouncement should have had such a damping effect. The Federal Trade Commission appears on the scene in 1915 with a frenetic burst of activity, perhaps attributable to a backlog of complaints; and the FTC index drops precipitously over the next fifteen years to the commencement of the depression. The sharp rise and then fall in the indexes of both the DOJ and the FTC during the 1930s and early 1940s is more a manifestation of the precipitous decline in real GNP followed by recovery than of an absolute increase in the number of cases brought. In more recent years these indexes have not changed dramatically.

The index pertaining to private cases is, in some ways, more interesting. It moves upward gradually from the date of the Sherman Act until the date when the Rule of Reason pronouncement might be thought to have had its effect. It then declines gradually until the mid-twenties, a date which I associate with the commencement of radio broadcasting and widespread auto-

Table 1-3
Numerical Data—Antitrust Cases

Dates	GNP (1958 dollars) [a]	DOJ Won [b]	DOJ Lost [b]	DOJ Total [b]	DOJ Index [c]	FTC Order [d]	FTC Dismiss [d]	FTC Total [d]	FTC Index [e]	Reported Private Cases [f]	Private Reported Index [g]
1890–1894	56.3	3	5	8	142					2	36
1895–1899	54.6	4	3	7	128					4	73
1900–1904	85.9	5	1	6	70					8	93
1905–1909	106	21	17	38	358					20	189
1910–1914	105	61	30	91	867					22	211
1915–1919	138	31	12	43	311	55	151	206	1490	17	123
1920–1924	149	42	24	66	443	40	136	176	1180	17	114
1925–1929	191	53	4	57	298	20	31	51	267	13	68
1930–1934	159	23	6	29	182	18	18	36	231	20	126
1935–1939	193	45	12	57	295	102	37	139	720	34	175
1940–1944	297	173	50	223	751	80	25	105	354	61	205
1945–1949	325	131	28	159	489	31	16	47	145	82	252
1950–1954	391	135	22	157	402	43	12	55	141	184	471
1955–1959	452	176	18	194	429	66	27	93	206	286	644
1960–1964	529	180	31	211	399	54	15	69	130	321	607
1965–1969	677	144	10	154	227	66	7	63	109	592	894
1970–1974	778	186	25	211	271	60	6	66	101	1260	1620
1975[h]	852	94	11	105	123	25	1	26	38.5	943	1107

a GNP averaged over 5-year period, all expressed in 1958 dollars $\times 10^{-9}$.

b Department of Justice data computed from CCH, the Federal Antitrust Laws With Summary of Cases Instituted by the United States 1890–1951 (1952); 1952–1956 Supp. (1957); Trade Reg. Rep. 10th ed., Transfer Binder, New U.S. Antitrust Cases (1957–61); 5 Trade Reg. Rep. (through 1977).

c Col. 5 ÷ col. 2 $\times 10^{-3}$; that is, cases per trillion dollars GNP in 1958 dollars.

d Federal Trade Commission data computed from FTC Dockets of Complaints; FTC Decisions (through 1975).

e Col. 9 ÷ col. 2 $\times 10^{-3}$; that is, cases per trillion GNP in 1958 dollars.

f Reported private cases for each year after 1963 are estimated from the number commenced in the year based on the relationship between reported and commenced private cases in 1963. Private Antitrust cases data computed from Nolo Contendere and Private Antitrust Enforcement, Hearings on S.2512, Subcommittee on Antitrust and Monopoly of the Senate Committee on the Judiciary, 89th Cong., 2d Sess., app. I, 180–324 (1966); United States Courts, Administrative Office, Annual Reports (through 1977).

g Col. 11 ÷ col. 2 $\times 10^{-3}$; that is, cases per trillion GNP in 1958 dollars.

h The GNP, DOJ statistics and reported private cases statistics are for the period 1975–1977. The FTC statistics are for the period 1975. The FTC Index was calculated using the GNP for that period (805).

mobile ownership and hence with a shift in scale economies in many industries. From that date it rises continuously, slowly through the end of the second World War and more rapidly to the mid 1960s. I am inclined to attribute the rapid rise after 1950 to the commencement of television broadcasting and also to the great uncertainty introduced into private antitrust litigation by the Supreme Court's 1946 decision in the *Bigelow* case.

Posner also speculates that this increase may be associated with the *Bigelow* decision but does so on the grounds that this dramatic change in the law of antitrust damages was very favorable to plaintiffs. Although, in my view, a change in doctrine favorable or unfavorable to plaintiffs should not cause the index to rise or fall in most instances (it should merely change the magnitude of judgments and of settlements), the *Bigelow* decision changed doctrine regarding proof of damages in a way that increased D, which might increase the index. A substantial infusion of uncertainty, on the other hand, should increase litigation because it is conducive to disparity in the estimates by parties as to the probability that liability will be found or the magnitude of damages likely to be awarded in the event of liability. That is, it facilitates a wide divergence between P_p and P_d, or between D_p and D_d.

In the years after 1966, the date of the class action amendments discussed previously, the index increases very sharply, an increase I attribute to that procedural change.

These aggregate case numbers appear to be inconsistent with the bureaucratic hypothesis and to be neutral with respect to the public-interest hypothesis and the private-bar hypothesis. To the extent that my spatial competition model of the interaction between large and small businesses is valid, the index numbers appear to support the small-business hypothesis in that they suggest antitrust enforcement is dramatically responsive to availability of the class-action vehicle.

In figure 1-2 I have added another time series to those shown on figure 1-1, namely an index of business failures. From time to time I have entertained yet a fifth hypothesis—perhaps it should be regarded as a modified small-business hypothesis—that the primary beneficiaries of antitrust were the creditors of failed firms. If business failure rates explain any significant part of antitrust activity, the failure index should move with the private activity index, perhaps leading it by a year or two, in many time periods. But I see no such relationship between the two series; indeed my casual inspection suggests a negative correlation.

Securities Prices

To most antitrust scholars, mindful of the work that has been done in recent years using securities prices to study the effects of mergers, an obvious place to start on the exploration of the hypotheses posed in the first section would be securities prices. Although recourse to the information implicit in securities prices was my first thought on embarking on this paper, that avenue appeared to me less and less attractive as I considered the problem further. So far as I am aware, securities prices available in machine readable form exist only for a relatively small number of firms and these are all firms of quite substantial size. Securities price data for a much wider set of firms are available in printed form. But even this larger set contains very few firms that I would be inclined to think of as typifying "small business"; and the smaller the firm of interest, the less likely there is to be a continuously active marketmaker for its shares. Morover, empirical work employing securities prices is largely dependent on the validity of the efficient market hypothesis; and as security markets become thin and trades sporadic, the validity of that thesis, by its own terms, is more and more open to doubt.

Preliminary to my contemplated endeavor to explore some aspect of the proposed hypotheses about antitrust using securities prices, I worked my way through the array of typical antitrust problems in an endeavor to identify several problems suitable for analysis through securities prices. In the end, I did no empiric work along these lines. But it may be marginally useful to recount the obstacles I foresaw in each of a variety of antitrust contexts.

Consider the classic section 2 case—a single firm which has established unambiguous dominance of an enduring kind in a nontrivial economic market. If the only existent rivalry is through cross-elasticity with some set of functionally distinguishable products (we can think of the *Cellophane* case as an illustration), what observations on security prices would be viewed as corroborating, or as inconsistent with, one of the hypotheses?

The public-interest hypothesis supposes that the dominant firm, after due process has been accorded, will be surgically divided into efficiently organized but thereafter rivalrous subparts. The exploitive monopoly phase now having been brought to an end, the aggregate market value of securities outstanding from the subparts should be observably less than the aggregate market value of the outstanding securities of the prelitigation monopoly.

The first difficulty is that the category itself comes close to being a null set. Dupont won the *Cellophane* case. Neither Alcoa nor United Machinery was dismembered in any significant sense. When the Standard Oil Trust was broken up many years ago, it was subdivided into a series of discrete regional enterprises that arguably has as much monopoly power in the aggregate as the prelitigation trust had had; and further, the compustat tapes of security prices do not go back so far.

But quite apart from these difficulties, the securities price history of the monopoly and of its surviving parts would not help us distinguish among the several hypotheses. All of the hypotheses would predict that the postlitigation securities value of the monopoly enterprise would fall. Indeed those

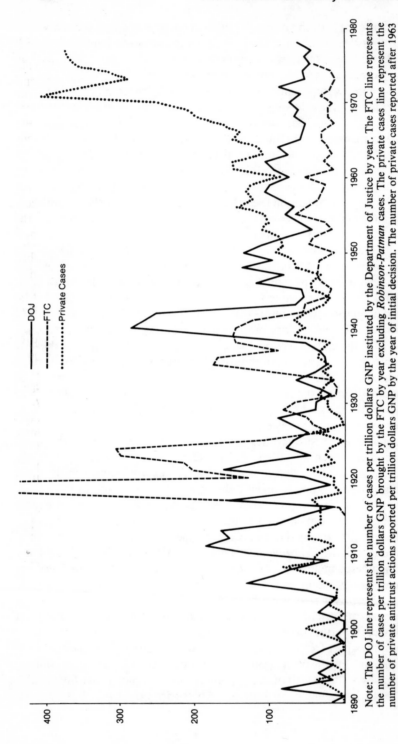

Figure 1-1. Antitrust Litigation Activity Normalized by GNP

Note: The DOJ line represents the number of cases per trillion dollars GNP instituted by the Department of Justice by year. The FTC line represents the number of cases per trillion dollars GNP brought by the FTC by year excluding *Robinson-Patman* cases. The private cases line represent the number of private antitrust actions reported per trillion dollars GNP by the year of initial decision. The number of private cases reported after 1963 is estimated from the number commenced based on the relationship of reported commenced cases in 1963.

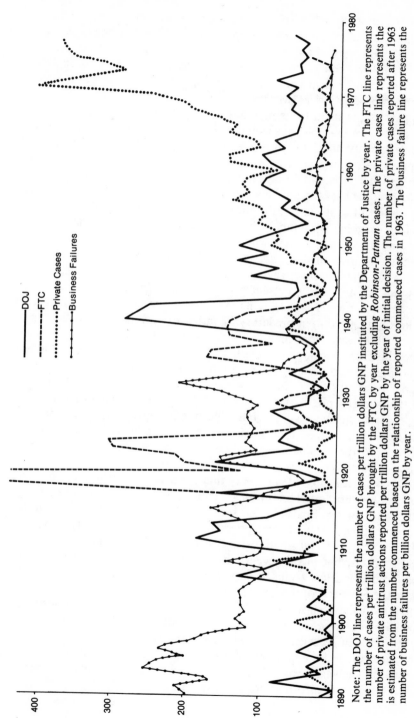

Note: The DOJ line represents the number of cases per trillion dollars GNP instituted by the Department of Justice by year. The FTC line represents the number of cases per trillion dollars GNP brought by the FTC by year excluding *Robinson-Patman* cases. The private cases line represents the number of private antitrust actions reported per trillion dollars GNP by the year of initial decision. The number of private cases reported after 1963 is estimated from the number commenced based on the relationship of reported commenced cases in 1963. The business failure line represents the number of business failures per billion dollars GNP by year.

Figure 1–2. Antitrust Litigation Activity and Business Failures Normalized by GNP

prices would likely fall further if the dismemberment is viewed as a side-show, incidental to the enrichment of the antitrust bar, or the expansion of the public sector, or as an anticompetitive device to improve the fortunes of small peripheral competitors. What we would need to know to be able to distinguish among hypotheses is something about the inflation-corrected pattern of product prices over the long run, or something about the securities prices of the small firms previously competing at the periphery. In the *Alcoa* Case, for example, one would want to look not only at the history of Alcoa's security prices but at the security prices of the set of firms which produced secondary aluminum. The public-interest hypothesis predicts these security prices should fall; the small-business hypothesis predicts they should rise; the bar- and public-sector hypotheses predict, over a set of such cases, no significant change. But the price series are unavailable.

The foregoing paragraph is implicitly addressed to the perhaps mytho-logical monopoly situation in which there is a single dominant firm engaging in exploitation of the inelastic demand curve over a substantial period and not simultaneously engaging in predatory behavior. Consider instead the situation, arguably represented by the *Shoe Machinery* case, in which the dominant firm is exploiting its inelastic demand curve in a number of markets but engaging in predatory or rather exclusionary behavior in par-ticular submarkets from time to time, presumably as new firms or newly vulnerable firms appear in those submarkets. The public-interest hypothesis would predict that security prices for the dominant firm should fall, that security prices for those firms at which predation was directed should rise and that security prices of established peripheral firms not jeopardized by the predatory behavior should fall. The small business hypothesis predicts that the security prices of all firms except the dominant firms should rise and those of the dominant firms should fall. Again, the critical data per-tains to the security prices of the peripheral firms.

Of course it is possible in theory that the peripheral firms are not small firms but are substantial ones with securities actively traded on an exchange or over the counter. But if they are substantial firms, how do we account for the fact that they are merely peripheral in the market under study? One pos-sibility is that their substantial size is accounted for by their activities in other markets; but in that event, the alteration of their prospects in the monopolized market would be very difficult to isolate from factors influ-encing the prospects of those firms in their principal markets.

Note further that it is essential to hypothesis testing that there be firms which are not jeopardized by the asserted predatory practices; for it is only the drop in their securities prices which enables us to distinguish between the public-interest and the small-business-subsidy hypotheses. It is not clear to me that any such case exists. I very much doubt that a sufficient number of such cases exists to afford an adequate sample size.

Consider as candidates for investigation cases involving horizontal price-fixing or other forms of asserted horizontal collusion. If all the firms in the industry are members of the conspiracy, then all share prices should drop as a result of enforcement; and this is true whether the asserted behavior is allocatively inefficient, as minimum price-fixing almost inevitably is, or whether the behavior is efficient, as basing point pricing or the exchange of data among competitors might well be. The validity of the two pertinent hypotheses can be distinguished, once again, only if there are peripheral firms not directly affected by the judicial relief awarded. The public-interest hypothesis predicts that security prices for those peripheral firms should fall; the small-business-subsidy hypothesis predicts that they should rise. In this context, too, assembling the pertinent data appears to be a formidable task.

When we shift attention from the classic horizontal cases to those typically characterized as vertical, the prospects for successful employment of securities prices to test the hypotheses do not appear to be much brighter. For the purposes immediately at hand, we need not distinguish resale price maintenance, territorial restrictions, and customer restrictions and exclusive dealing arrangements. In all three categories, antitrust attack is appropriate if the practice is being employed, as it may conceivably be, to facilitate cartel administration at the upstream level or to facilitate monopolistic behavior at the downstream level. Alternatively, antitrust attack is unwarranted and inefficient if the practice is being employed by individual manufacturers to minimize the occurrence of downstream free-rider behavior that interferes with the efficient provision by downstream parties of information or other free-rider susceptible services.

The expected shifts in security prices under the two pertinent hypotheses across these three different types of cases are as follows:

1. The public-interest hypothesis would predict that antitrust attack on an arrangement which actually involved collusion at the upstream level would cause a fall in security prices for manufacturers in the market, both those that were and those that were not employing the vertical practice; it is unclear whether the securities prices of retailers who had agreed to the apparently vertical restraint should be expected to rise because of volume increases, to remain unchanged because the products line affected was not a significant part of their inventories, or to fall because they are no longer being paid off by the manufacturers for accepting the restriction. Securities of competing retailers, never subject to the restrictions but carrying competing lines, should fall.

2. In the case of an apparently vertical restriction being used to facilitate cartelization at the retail level, the public-interest theory would predict that securities prices of retailers, both those that had agreed to the restriction and their competitors who had not, would fall; whereas the securities

of manufacturers might rise on volume increases, remain unchanged if the product line were of minor significance, or fall if payoffs from the retailers have been lost. Securities of manufacturers, not involved but selling competing lines, should fall.

3. The small-business hypothesis implies that a large fraction of litigation over these apparently vertical practices involve arrangements intended to eliminate free-rider problems and having no relationship to cartel behavior at either the upstream or the downstream level. If cases of that type do in fact make up the preponderance of cases, then the securities prices of the manufacturers employing the agreements and the retailers who were parties to the agreement should fall; whereas security prices of rival manufacturers and of rival retailers should rise or remain constant.

Thus it appears that using securities prices to test the public-interest hypothesis in these antitrust contexts, while theoretically possible, is likely to be very difficult. As before, it is not clear how securities prices would assist in distinguishing between the small-business hypothesis, the organized antitrust bar hypothesis, and the public-sector hypothesis—all three, in the present context, predict merely that cases will be brought without regard for the effects on the ultimate consumer and without regard to the probability that cartel behavior at one level or another is being facilitated. Thus even effective use of testing procedure perhaps could do no more than reject the public-interest hypothesis. Even if a hypothesis other than the public-interest one is accurate, there is no reason to think that the resultant antitrust apparatus would select against cases that did involve cartel facilitating behavior at one or the other levels, so that the resulting set of cases is likely to be mixed in some unknown proportions. Still, given adequate sample size, I would expect the test successfully to distinguish between the public-interest and the alternative hypotheses, for the predicted movements of securities prices are markedly different.

The practical requirements for a securities prices test of the public-interest hypothesis thus appear to be the ability to identify a sufficient number of industries in which (a) some vertical restriction, or preferably some particular subtype of vertical restriction has been challenged, (b) some but less than all the sellers (buyers) in the industry had been using the restriction, (c) the product line was a significant fraction of the commercial activity of each of the sellers (buyers), and (d) an adequate record of public trading exists over a period of several years before and after the challenge for the securities of some of the sellers (buyers) who were and some of the sellers (buyers) who were not using the restriction.

With respect to the last of the traditional vertical categories, tie-in sales, it seems to me highly unlikely that observations of security prices could be of any assistance in distinguishing among the relevant hypotheses. An initial difficulty is that the tie-in cases do not, in fact, form a single category but rather four or more conceptually distinct categories. Furthermore, it is unknown how frequently ties of any one of the four types are used; and, more importantly, it is unknowable how frequently ties of each of the types would be used were it not for the sweeping legal prohibition against the use of any type. A more fundamental difficulty is that the security price movements which are to be expected in each category as a consequence of successful enforcement, and which would help us distinguish between the several hypotheses, are unclear.

One category of cases to which few economically literate observers would choose to apply the tie-in prohibition (at least if this were the only category so that no argument could be made on the basis of simplicity in favor of an all encompassing rule) is that category in which a seller imposes the condition that a second product be bought because the tie is the minimum transaction cost device for achieving quality control and minimizing downstream free-rider behavior. Although not all the franchise cases which involve tie-in requirements fall in this category, many do; and they can be taken as a paradigm of the category. A franchisor establishes a trademark and promotes it nationally aiming at a customer set which is peripatetic and risk averse. The nominal product is hamburgers, or fried chicken, or overnight accommodations; but from the standpoint of the aggregate enterprise, a very important characteristic of the product is that both its quality and its price in Yakima are the same as those the wandering American family has experienced and found satisfactory to its taste and budget back home in Paducah. It is not necessary to the successful execution of this concept that the quality be high or that the prices be low; what is necessary is that they are at the level the customer has previously found satisfactory and has come to associate with the trademark. The standardization of logos, personnel uniforms, outlet architecture, and golden arches are all intended to convey to the travelers information—reassurance that he will not find to his horror that the least expensive dinner on the menu which his four children will eat is coq au vin at $5.95 a plate or, alternatively, that the 95¢ hamburgers are so small that the children will be clamoring to eat again in an hour.

But there is no assurance in these circumstances that the particular combinations of price and quality that will be profit maximizing for the aggregate national enterprise will be maximizing in the particular local market of an individual franchisee; and the franchisee's incentive may be strong to adopt a different combination, thus maximizing against his local customer set while free-riding on the national trademark to the extent that he captures some customers from afar. It is of little consequence to him that his local deviance subverts the confident expectations of travelers and thus undermines the central promotional efforts of the franchisor; for today's disappointed traveler will not pass his way again soon. Other franchisees will bear the cost of defeated expectations.

If the franchisor requires the franchisee, in these circumstances, to buy his chicken and the grease in which it is to be fried from the franchisor or from an approved source, it is not, as the Supreme Court would have it, because the franchisor is attempting to "extend" his "trademark monopoly" to dressed poultry and vegetable oil. It is true, but irrelevant, that there will be other methods of quality control that are possible; there is no reason to think that the franchisor has adopted a method other than the most cost effective. Across the set of cases, there can be little doubt that prohibition of the tie will either force substitution of a more expensive method of assuring standardization or lead to abandonment of that effort. From the standpoint of consumers, both results are adverse; either consumer prices rise or the richness of the product set available to the consumer is diminished.

It is true, of course, that a tie of this type can be used to make covert redistribution of rents in favor of the franchisor; but the franchisor's flexibility in this respect is sharply limited to the magnitude of the franchisee's locational rents; the industries involved are intensely competitive in all but the smallest communities, and no allocatively significant monopoly profits can be earned in this way.

If the tie is prohibited in this context, what is to be expected of securities prices? Those of the franchisor will fall, but that is of no help in distinguishing between hypotheses; for the securities prices of the seller who imposes a tie will fall under all hypotheses if a prohibition is applied. If information is to be gained, it must be gained from the securities prices of the franchisees, but the behavior of these prices will be quite complex. Those of the most successful free-riders, those whose local profit maximizing price-quality combinations are most disparate from the nationally maximizing combination, should rise in the short run. Those of other franchisees should remain unchanged for some indeterminate period of time and then fall as the effects of the free-rider behavior set in. In the long run, all franchisees revert to the status of individual local competitors in an intensely competitive environment. Presumably they have no comparative advantage in that environment and many will have a distinct comparative disadvantage since location, size, and many other parameters of their production function were not selected with reference to that environment. Hence in the aggregate franchisee security prices should fall in the long run.

Clearly such short and long run behavior of franchisee security prices, if indeed securities prices exist in any traditional sense, would be exceedingly difficult to observe. But if it could be observed, what inferences should be drawn from it? Perhaps it could be taken as confirming a motivation on the part of policy makers to favor small business; equally certainly that has not been the result. It does not confirm the public-interest hypothesis, but it might be thought to confirm a modified small business hypothesis, which has as a feature persistently erroneous expectations. That price pattern does support either or both the private bar and the public sector hypotheses.

I turn to another, I think by far the most numerous, category of tie-in cases: the tie used to meter demand elasticity and achieve price discrimination. Application of the rule in this context depresses the security prices of the seller, as is always true; it should enhance the securities prices of that set of buyers who previously paid prices above the uniform, profit maximizing, monopoly price which the seller will charge subsequent to successful enforcement, and it will depress the securities prices of those buyers who previously paid less. Again, even if the necessary set of securities prices was available for observation, it seems that no useful inferences can be drawn. The controversy over these applications of the tie-in rule does not involve disagreements about the way in which the immediate parties are affected but about the long run impact on consumers. In my judgment, the long run effect on consumers will be adverse in a great preponderance of circumstances; but there are those who disagree. But it seems clear that observation of securities prices of immediate parties cannot resolve that controversy and hence can shed no light on the public-interest hypothesis. Security price observations might inform us whether large or small buyers were consistently disadvantaged to the advantage of the other. Hence it might throw some light on the small-business hypothesis; but one of the oddities about this group of tie-in cases is that it seems intuitively probable that it is large buyers rather than small who, in these cases, typically have more intense demands for the tying product and from whom rents (or surplus) are drawn away.

A third type of tie-in case is that in which the seller engages in disguised price competition by providing some complimentary good or service at a price less than the competitive price; the *Fortner* case is an illustration. Again the impact of enforcement on the immediate parties to such transactions seems clear enough: the securities of both the defendant seller and his buyers should be negatively affected (although the adverse effects on particular buyers may be ameliorated or even totally offset to the extent of their ability to recover treble damages from their seller). The securities prices of competing sellers, whose prices were being undercut, should be increased; and the effects on those who bought from those competing sellers should be negative although perhaps of insufficient magnitude to be observable. I assume that substantially all would agree that application of the tying rule to cases of this type is allocatively perverse, and hence the mere existence of this set of cases tends to reject the public interest hypothesis. Note that the pattern of price movements is the same as that which is to be expected in the first category of tie-in cases, also allocatively perverse, involving quality control and free-rider effects.

It seems possible but not probable that there are systematic size differences between those sellers who gain and those who lose, or between those buyers who gain and those buyers who lose, from the enforcement of the tying rule in this context. If we were to find that large sellers engage in this type of price competition and that large buyers were its immediate beneficiaries, then the predicted securities prices observations would tend to support the small-business hypothesis very strongly. But observations on buyer security prices would be essential to such a conclusion, for the general pattern of securities price movements expected on the part of seller firms does not distinguish this category of tie-in case from any of the other categories.

The final category of tie-in cases, and the only one in which legal prohibition is defensible in my view in terms of allocative efficiency, consists of those cases in which a seller with a major market share for the tying product is successful, by means of a tie, in capturing a major market share of the tied product. Although in static terms the device is allocatively neutral, there may well be circumstances in which the dynamic consequences would be to deter entry by other firms, either into the market for the tying product (the tie of repair services to shoe machinery by United Shoe Machinery might be an example) or into the market for the tied product for a time period exceeding the expected duration of market power in the tying market (the *Motion Picture Patents* case may be an example). Again the expected securities price movements are fairly clear—downward for the defendant sellers; upward for competing sellers, if indeed there are any; and upward for buyers, although possibly only with considerable lag. Again observations on buyer prices are critical, and the unknown duration of lag is likely to make interpretation difficult even if the necessary price series are available.

In my judgment the basic question about the validity of a sweeping tie-in prohibition, and the information which security price movements would yield with respect to the several hypotheses, does not turn on the impacts within the individual categories but rather on the economic significance of the categories. I think that most observers will agree that the first and third categories have socially perverse impacts. Hence, if one could show that cases of those types predominate in the total set of tie-in cases, this would constitute strong evidence against the public interest hypothesis. But those cases cannot be distinguished from the metering cases by securities price observations alone. The price movements in the quality control cases and the metering cases are substantially the same.

For one who shares my point of view that all of the categories are socially perverse with the exception of the last, that involving preemption of the tied-product market, observation on buyer's prices across the set of tie-in cases would provide evidence, although only weak evidence, on the public-interest hypothesis. A strong upward movement in buyer security prices would tend to confirm the hypothesis; any other result would tend to reject it. Nevertheless this evidence would be weak because different sets of buyers are differentially affected both in the metering cases and the quality control cases; and it is not inevitable that those two pairs of impacts will cancel one another out.

The one remaining set of cases to be discussed are those based on the

Robinson-Patman Act. A subset of these, namely the primary line cases, are amenable to the same tests discussed in conjunction with predatory pricing. The remainder, the secondary line cases under 2(a) and all cases arising under (c), (d), and (e), appear to have similar effects and to be amenable to analysis as a single group. The 2(f) cases include cases of both primary line and secondary line types; those involving beneficiaries of primary line discrimination should also be viewed as predatory pricing cases and the remainder put into the pool with the rest of *Robinson-Patman* cases.

Once again, and for very much the same reasons as have been given before, observations on security prices seem to me unlikely to be of much utility for testing secondary line cases against the several hypotheses. Security prices of offending sellers should fall in the short run under all hypotheses; those of buyers who were the beneficiaries of price discrimination should fall, those of buyers who compete with the beneficiaries should rise. But this much is obvious from a casual reading of the Act. More information would be yielded if it proved to be the case that systematic size differences existed between the two sets of buyers. If the buyers who did not receive the benefits of discrimination were systematically smaller enterprises, then a rise in their security prices would tend to confirm the small business hypothesis. Even under those circumstances we would learn nothing about the public-interest hypothesis. In this context, too, only long run observations on prices of consumer goods and services would answer that question.

The one important category of antitrust cases not yet discussed is the merger category. Here, for several reasons, observations on security prices seems to me to afford a much more promising avenue of investigation than in other categories. There are several reasons for this: first, because the rules applicable are of the Rule-of-Reason type, many mergers are legal and hence many mergers occur in open and well-documented forms. Second, many of the firms who participated in mergers are substantial firms with significant market shares with the consequence that their behavior will often affect significantly the industries in which they operate. Third, and perhaps most importantly, many of the merger participants have as their competitors other substantial firms whose securities are actively traded and have readily available price histories. These reasons no doubt account, at least in part, for the fact that mergers constitute the area in which most securities price studies have been conducted.

While these comments seem to me accurate with respect to mergers of all types prior to 1950 and continue to be accurate with respect to conglomerate mergers, they may be less accurate with respect to horizontal and vertical mergers as of some date between the passage of the Celler-Kefauver Act of 1950 and the Supreme Court's decision in the *Brown Shoe* case in 1962. It is difficult to assign any precise date after which prospective merger partners began anticipating the draconian interpretation imposed by the

Warren Court on amended Section 7 with respect to horizontal and vertical mergers; but clearly mergers that were predominantly horizontal or vertical and which involved substantial market shares must have declined significantly after the early 1960s. Nevertheless is seems likely that adequate data exists from the 1950s and earlier to support interesting and instructive studies on vertical and horizontal mergers on the basis of securities prices. And perhaps there are sufficient number of vertical mergers, and of mergers that are substantially horizonal in their effects such as geographical extension mergers from more recent periods to make such studies, too, worthwhile undertakings. Obviously enormous bodies of data pertaining to mergers that are predominantly conglomerate are readily available.

What I found somewhat surprising in my less than thorough canvass of securities price studies of mergers was that substantially all are addressed to conglomerate mergers and substantially all focus attention on the history of the securities prices of the merging parties. Typically, these studies ask the question whether the aggregate value of securities outstanding by the postmerger firm is greater or less than the combined value of the securities of the two individual firms prior to the merger. This is a perfectly sensible question to ask in the context of conglomerate mergers although, even in that context, not the only question of interest. Certainly with respect to horizontal and vertical mergers, and perhaps with respect to conglomerate mergers as well, more interesting and possibly more definitive results might be obtained by focusing on competitors of the merging firms rather than on the firms themselves.

Let us suppose that it was possible to assemble securities price data for a group of twenty or thirty horizontal mergers of substantial size from the pre-1950 period. In this context, an increase in the combined securities value of the merger partners would not be an unambiguous result. It might indicate that the combined firms had achieved cost savings or other efficiencies as a consequence of merger, but alternatively it might indicate that the resultant increase in concentration in the industry had facilitated successful cartelization. Far more interesting would be the pattern of securities prices of competitors of these firms. If the primary effect of the merger was attainment of efficiencies and more vigorous competition, securities prices of rival firms should fall; whereas the cartelization explanation should be revealed by increases.

These relationships are too obvious to have escaped widespread notice, yet I am unaware of any work done along these lines. Perhaps this is because the general validity of the antitrust restriction on horizontal mergers is one of the least controversial of all antitrust laws. Such controversy as there is pertains to the level of market concentration at which horizontal mergers become a concern. And of course enormous numbers of studies have approached that question more directly by studying the correlation between concentration and profitability.

Nevertheless, it seems to me, even in the context of horizontal mergers, investigations of this kind would be highly useful. Work demonstrating the statistical association between concentration and profitability is open to a serious cause-and-effect question, one that has been effectively pressed by Professors Demsetz and Brozen among others. That would not seem to be true of an investigation along the lines proposed.

Very much the same type of studies would be revealing in the context of vertical mergers as well, where there is a good deal more controversy about the validity of antitrust restrictions. It is my understanding that even those who would defend stringent restrictions on vertical mergers are agreed that such adverse effects as such mergers may cause derive ultimately from effective increases in horizontal concentration at either the upper or the lower functional level. Although it is argued that there may be foreclosure effects on certain other firms, if the overall effect of a vertical merger is significantly to increase concentration at one level or the other, then the general pattern of competitor's security prices should be upward. If the mergers are preponderantly efficiency enhancing, the general pattern of competitor's securities price movement should be downward. It seems likely that there is a sufficient number of instances of vertical mergers in industries populated by competitors whose shares are actively traded so that investigation along these lines would be feasible.

Studies on the securities prices of competitors of the two merging firms in the conglomerate merger context, too, seem likely to yield new insights. Like the area of vertical mergers, commentators who frequently see dangers in conglomerate mergers offer a variety of reasons why adverse consequences will follow. These reasons, in my judgment, range from the quite plausible to totally fanciful; but there is no need to have any particular view on the plausibility of these concerns in order to state the pattern of security price movements which, if the concerns have substance, would be expected to characterize competing enterprises.

Perhaps the most frequent objection to conglomerate mergers is that one of the merging firms is a potential entrant into the industry of the other via an avenue more likely than the merger route to intensify competition. If the public interest hypothesis is to be supported, examination of a set of such mergers attacked but not successfully blocked by enforcement officials should reveal an upward trend in competitor security prices; and in cases where the merger was successfully blocked, securities prices of competitors should trend upward from a point at or before the merger announcement and then downward after the outcome of antitrust enforcement became apparent. If such cases are brought predominantly to provide employment for government officials or on the complaint of competitors who hope to be sheltered from the consequence of mergers they expect to be efficiency enhancing, price patterns should be the opposite—downward where the merger is not successfully blocked, upward where it is.

In mergers attacked on one or the other of the closely related grounds of "entrenchment" or "deep-pocket effects," there may be some ambiguity about the direction of competitor's security prices immediately following the announcement of a merger suspect on those grounds. Conceivably commentators who find these lines of argument appealing might expect the intimidation effects of the merger to extend as far as the security holders of competitive firms, resulting in a short-run down turn. But it seems to me that if any serious attempt to defend restrictions on the basis of these arguments is to be made, it must be conceded that competitors' security prices will rise after a period of a year or two. These theories depict competitors as terrorized into passivity, but the passivity must necessarily be of an enriching kind if it is to be maintained that the intensity of competition in the market has been reduced.

Objections based on recognized mutual interdependence can be tested with respect to the same expected patterns. Restrictions survive the public-interest test if the security prices of competitors move upward when such mergers are unsuccessfully challenged and downward where the challenge prevails. Opposite movements would lend support to one or another or all of the rival hypotheses.

A final category of conglomerate merger to which objection is made is that involving the prospect of reciprocity. It is not clear to me whether anyone seriously takes the position that this objection can be based on allocative considerations. Rather, the argument seems to be that it is unfair for some companies to be able to compete through these price disguising mechanisms while other companies are forced to respond by reducing price, by improving quality, or by other traditional means. But if the argument extends to the point of supposing that some of the "foreclosed" competitors are actually pushed out of the market, thus increasing concentration and facilitating cartel behavior, then this proposition, too, is susceptible to the tests previously described. If no firms are excluded, I fail to see how competition could be lessened.

Political Voting Patterns

In this part I will describe a line of empiric research which I once hoped to undertake in time to allow the results to form a major portion of the present paper. A series of frustrating failures to obtain the necessary data in forms that were practical had the consequence that I have no results at all to report. Nevertheless I continue to regard the line of inquiry as potentially the most promising attack on the central questions to which the paper is addressed.

Basically my original goal was to do regression analysis, using as dependent variables the yes and no roll-call votes of individual congressmen in the House of Representatives at the time of the passage of the Sherman, Clayton, Robinson-Patman, and Celler-Kefauver Acts; and I intended to use as independent variables an assortment of demographic and economic data pertaining to their individual congressional districts. I now know that investigation along these lines is, to a limited extent, quite feasible but that, except to that limited extent, pursuit of this line of inquiry would be extremely expensive, time-consuming, and perhaps impossible. In the following paragraphs, for the purpose of stimulating discussion of whether the general approach is worth further efforts and for the purpose of facilitating such efforts by others, I will first report briefly on the results on my inquiry into the availability of data and next on what I think might usefully be done with that data which is, and which over the years ahead will become, readily available.

Obtaining the necessary data with respect to roll-call votes poses no problem. This data is available on computer tapes for each roll-call vote over the entire historic period; and the data is organized so that all the roll-call votes of an individual Congress (that is, 81st Congress, 1st and 2nd Sessions) are contained in one particular tape and the roll-call votes of each Congress is contained on a separate tape. These tapes can be obtained from the Interuniversity Consortium for Political and Social Research (IUCPSR) headquartered at the University of Michigan. (Telephone: (313) 763–5010). For the purpose of identification, each individual congressman who has served in the Congress has been assigned a separate number which identifies him.

Somewhat more difficult is the process of associating a particular congressman with a particular piece of geography, that is a particular group of counties in a particular state; but my preliminary efforts along these lines lead me to believe that this probably can be done without great difficulty for all Congresses since that which enacted the Sherman Act. (The *Congressional Directory* contains such geographic descriptions for all members.)

A far more serious obstacle, however, to pursuing this line of investigation with respect to the principal antitrust enactments is that census data which associates useful economic variables with small geographic subdivisions of the United States proved to be unavailable for any period prior to 1940. Hence, while it would be rash to say it would be impossible for anyone to assemble sufficient economic data on a congressional-district-by-congressional-district basis prior to 1940, that task would certainly represent an enormous project involving resort to records not presently aggregated in any single place, much less any small collection of volumes.

Starting shortly after the 1940 census, the Census Bureau began associating data pertaining to a fairly rich set of economic variables with small geographic areas, first for Standard Metropolitan Areas,[2] and somewhat later, 1947, for individual counties.[3] Hence, it would be a somewhat less heroic project to pursue this line of inquiry for Congresses elected in 1940 and thereafter. Nevertheless, the project would be very substantial. First, there is some doubt how much of this data for counties is available in machine readable form.[4] At a minimum, the 3,000-odd counties in the United States would have to be assigned to 435 congresssional districts as they existed from 1940 to 1950 and the county data aggregated into congressional district data. And any needed county data not available in machine readable form would have to be manually punched and verified for each of the 3,000-odd counties and then aggregated by district.

The next installment of the *County and City Data Book* appeared in 1956, based on the 1950 census and the 1954 census of business. The same comments made above regarding the 1947 publication apply to this volume too. Investigation based on the 1956 data, although no less arduous, is more tempting because a far richer set of variables for each county are covered. For example, data pertaining to income appears for the first time, and data pertaining to the number of proprietors of unincorporated businesses is included for a larger number of industrial sectors than was true in the earlier edition.

The *County and City Data Book for 1956* does contain some data aggregated by congressional districts. But in contrast to the 133 variables listed for each county, very few variables of any interest to the contemplated investigation are covered on a district basis. And the number of congressional districts for which any data is published is incomplete and distinctly biased in the direction of rural districts. Only districts composed of one or more entire counties are listed.

The *County and City Data Book* is a continuing series published by the Bureau; another appeared in 1967, another in 1972. With each successive volume, the richness of the data included becomes greater. Moreover it is clear that all the data are available in machine-readable form for the year 1967 and subsequent years. Nevertheless I discuss the series no further because in the 1960s the Bureau began a new series in which data are presented on a congressional-district-by-congressional-district basis, thus greatly facilitating the type of inquiry under discussion. The first publication in this series, published in 1963, consists of an effort by the Bureau to aggregate the county data from the 1950s by congressional district as the districts were constituted pursuant to the 1950 census. The next volume in this series, the *Congressional District Data Book for the 88th Congress of 1963–65,* was based on the 1960 census; and again the richness of the data increases from a first volume to the second. Unfortunately neither the data in the first nor in the second of this series is anywhere available in machine-readable form.[5]

The first unambiguously good news pertains to the *Congressional District Data Book for the 93rd Congress [1973–75],* based on the 1970 census, for congressional districts constituted pursuant to that census. The data set is rich and it is available in machine readable form.

Unfortunately a very small fraction of existing antitrust legislation, and arguably none that is fundamental to the enterprise, was enacted by the 93rd or subsequent congresses. The Antitrust Procedures and Penalties Act was enacted by the 93rd Congress and the Antitrust Improvements Act of 1976 was enacted by the 94th. Accordingly, about the most that can be done along the line I had originally hoped would become the central portion of this paper, is to regress data from the most recent *Congressional District Data Book* against selected roll call votes on those two pieces of legislation.

Although ideally one would prefer to run the contemplated regressions on roll-call votes pertaining to the major pieces of antitrust legislation, there were two roll-call votes in the House in 1976 that would serve as very satisfactory vehicles for the contemplated investigation. The major issue in both these roll calls was the *parens patria* provisions authorizing state attorneys general to bring treble damage actions on behalf of consumers in their states. At this point in time the availability of any workable remedy for ultimate consumers was very much in doubt; and any congressman who thought that the antitrust laws, taken as a whole, conferred benefits on a constituency important to him would almost certainly have concluded that this remedial provision would increase the efficacy of the forces which yielded those benefits. Conversely, the motions before the House could hardly have been favored by one who thought the central thrust of those laws was damaging to an important constituency. Hence these two roll calls arguably can be viewed as a referendum on the very broad issue whether the overall effect of antitrust enforcement helped or hurt the members of a constituency. Moreover the number of members voting on each roll call was large, just under 400 in both instances.[6]

Against these roll-call votes it would be possible to regress a fair variety of independent variables drawn from the *Congressional District Data Book for the 93rd Congress*. Data which could be taken directly from the tapes include total population of the district, population per square mile, population broken down by central cities, urban, and rural categories, number of families with income in each of seven different brackets ranging from below $3,000 to over $25,000, number of persons employed by each federal, state, and local government, and the number of persons employed in each of eleven different subdivisions of the private sector.

Even this most recent *Congressional District Data Book* does not contain as rich a set of variables of interest as do recent editions of the *City County Data Book*. The latter, for example, contains such variables as value of farm shipments, value added by manufacture, and the number of unincorporated proprietorships in each of the variety of commercial sectors. Since the more recent City County Data Books are available in machine readable form, it would be possible to write a program, using the

Congressional District Data Book for guidance as to how the counties should be aggregated to form any particular congressional district, to aggregate these additional variables by machine and merge them with variables from the congressional district tape so as to form a still richer data set.

If the public-interest hypothesis holds, the income effects of antitrust enforcement must surely be egalitarian—the beneficiaries all are consumers; monopoly rents undoubtedly flow primarily to upper income groups. The hypothesis would be supported, then, if affirmative votes were strongly correlated with districts populated largely by lower-income groups. A negative correlation would tend to reject the public-interest hypothesis and to support the small-business hypothesis. The organized bar- and public-sector hypotheses, on the other hand, are consistent with the absence of any significant correlation with income levels.

One might expect to find that enthusiasm for public-sector expansion was particularly marked among public sector employees. A variable representing percentage of work force employed in the public sector is readily available.

Although in my view the small-business hypothesis is most tenable when the beneficiaries are conceived to be relatively small business on an industry by industry basis rather than absolutely small enterprises, the number of persons associated with relatively small business as well as with absolutely small business is probably greatest in the retail, wholesale and service sectors. The proportion of the work force employed in these sectors might serve adequately as a proxy for the political significance of these groups in any particular district. I think it likely that the number of unincorporated proprietorships, aggregated across all sectors, would constitute a better proxy, but this variable could be constructed only by employing the *City County Data Book*. Construction of a variable along one of these lines could be used further to test the small business hypothesis.

I can identify no variable present in any of the census data that seems likely to be of assistance in testing the organized bar hypothesis. Data pertaining to employment in the "professional" category is available; but lawyers represent a modest fraction of that category and antitrust lawyers represent an extremely small fraction. Even if the hypothesis is true, I would think it amazing if it were possible to reject the null hypothesis by employing these data.

Testimony at Congressional Hearings on Antitrust Bills

The final data set that I explore is the identity of witnesses who have physically appeared and testified before congressional committees during hearings preliminary to the major antitrust enactments from the Sherman Act in

1890 to the Antitrust Improvements Act of 1976. Persons testifying before congressional committees in the course of such hearings usually do so voluntarily and incur travel and preparation expenses in order to appear and testify. A priori, it seems possible to me that the identity of these witnesses might yield interesting information about who expects to win and to lose should pending bills be enacted.

After an initial scan of various hearings, I established a number of categories into which witnesses might be sorted. I then proceeded through the hearings which led to the passage of the Sherman Act, the Clayton Act, the Robinson-Patman Act, the Celler-Kefauver Amendment of 1950, and the Antitrust Improvements Act of 1976. The resultant data is presented in table 1-4.

No doubt the most striking feature of table 1-4 at first glance is that there are no entries under the Sherman Act. The reason for this is that the hearings which led to the passage of the Sherman Act were of wholly different character than any of the subsequent hearings. Indeed, there are no hearings at all (as opposed to committee reports and congressional debates) on the bill submitted by Senator Sherman or any predecessor bill. There were, however, quite extensive hearings on the trust phenomenon before the Committee on Manufactures in 1888 and 1889; and these hearings surely had a major influence on the passage of the Sherman Act. But these hearings were more nearly akin to a grand jury investigation than to the typical congressional hearing on pending legislation. Factual inquiry was made into the industrial history of the Sugar Trust, the Standard Oil Trust and the Whiskey Trust. The witnesses called were persons who were or had been employed in those industries, and the questions put to them were about facts within the witnesses' personal knowledge pertaining to one of those industries. Witnesses were not asked to, nor did they, express views on the desirability of the enactment of any particular legislation. Accordingly witnesses at those hearings cannot appropriately be counted as persons who

Table 1-4
Witnesses in Congressional Hearings

	Clayton Act	Robinson-Patman Act	Celler-Kefauver	A.T. Improvements
Politicians				
Pro	4/3.9	2/3.4	11/16.2	3/8.3
Con	4/3.9	0/0	0/0	1/2.8
Bureaucrats				
Pro	.5/.5	0/0	36/52.9	6/16.7
Con	.5/.5	0/0	0/0	1/2.8

Table 4–1 continued

	Clayton Act	Robinson-Patman Act	Celler-Kefauver	A.T. Improvements
Small business				
Pro	9.5/9.3	6.5/11.0	8/11.8	1.5/4.2
Con	2.5/2.5	4.5/7.6	1/1.5	0/0
Professional Consumer				
Pro	2.5/2.5	0/0	1/1.5	2/5.6
Con	3/2.9	1/1.7	0/0	0/0
Academic				
Pro	2/2.0	0/0	0/0	5/13.9
Con	2/2.0	0/0	0/0	1/2.8
Labor				
Pro	1.5/1.5	0/0	1/1.5	0/0
Con	0/0	2/3.4	0/0	0/0
Organized bar				
Pro	0/0	0/0	0/0	.5/1.4
Con	0/0	0/0	0/0	3.5/9.7
Lawyers				
Pro	5.5/5.4	0/0	0/0	6/16.7
Con	5.5/5.4	0/0	0/0	0/0
Exemptions	11.5/11.3	0/0	3/4.4	.5/1.4
Other private				
Pro	13.5/13.2	3/5.1	1/1.5	0/0
Con	34/33	40/67.8	6/8.8	5/13.8
Total number of witnesses	102	59	68	36

Note: The category *Politicians* includes all elected officials; with only trivial exceptions this category was composed of congressmen. *Bureaucrats* are composed of government employees other than elected officials. For the most part this category consisted of employees of the Antitrust Division or the Federal Trade Commission. Several state attorneys-general testified regarding the Antitrust Improvements Act. *Small business* is constituted of witnesses who explicitly invoked the term *small business* or a close synonym as the object of their concern or who identified themselves with organizations known to be representative of small business enterprises. *Professional consumer* is constituted of witnesses who explicitly associated themselves with grass-roots organizations purporting to represent consumers. *Academic* is constituted of persons who identified themselves as holding teaching positions at universities. *Labor* is constituted of persons who explicitly identified themselves as representing the labor movement. *Organized bar* is constituted of witnesses who represented themselves as authorized to express the views of the American Bar Association. *Lawyers* are constituted of persons who identified themselves as attorneys and purported to be speaking on their own behalf rather than on behalf of a client. *Exemptions* is constituted of witnesses whose major position on the pending bill was that the interest they represented should be exempted from its coverage. *Other private* is a residual category but is constituted predominantly of persons who explicitly identified themselves as presenting the position of some private company, some group of companies, or a trade association not known to be representative primarily of small business enterprises.

Each cell contains four entries: the top line in each cell indicates, first, the number of witnesses within the category who testified in favor of the bill and, second, the percentage which that number represents of the total number of witnesses who testified at the set of hearings. The second line in each cell indicates the number of witnesses who opposed enactment and the percentage of the total number of witnesses which this number represents.

thought it worth their while to incur travel and other expenses for the purpose of influencing the passage of legislation.

Hearings on the other four major pieces of legislation were of the traditional type. The numbers, however, are disappointing. I find nothing in them that lends unambiguous support to any one of the hypotheses. It does seem fair to say however that the numbers tend to refute both the public-sector hypothesis and the organized bar hypothesis.

Prior to the hearings on the 1976 legislation, no witnesses identified himself as spokesmen for the organized bar. In 1976, three out of the four who did so identify themselves were in substantial opposition to passage. A fourth, whom I counted half in favor and half against, took positions favorable to portions of the legislation and unfavorable to the balance.

Witnesses, who were identifiable as attorneys but did not purport to be appearing on behalf of some client, testified in the Clayton Act hearings and also in the 1976 hearings. But with respect to the Clayton Act, the testimony of these witnesses divided equally pro and con. It was not until 1976 that lawyers, identifiable as plaintiff's treble damage types, took a role in antitrust hearings. In 1976, six did appear and testify, all favorably.

So far as the public-sector hypothesis goes, it too founders, by the present test at least, on the very low participation rate of either politicians or bureaucrats among the witnesses. Moreover, with respect to the Clayton Act, as many testified in opposition as testified in favor. Except two statements by Congressman Patman, there were no such appearances in the course of the 1936 hearings. The Celler-Kefauver Hearings were exceptional in this respect: a number of congressmen did testify, all favorably. And at one subset of the hearings, a series of employees of the Federal Trade Commission paraded across the witness stand, each to present what purported to be a study of mergers in the context of some particular industry.

The only two categories of witnesses who appear in substantial numbers across the set of hearings are witnesses for small business and witnesses for other industrial sectors. Across the set of hearings, the small-business witnesses testified in favor of the legislation in over 75 percent of the instances. Witnesses from the Other Private category, on the other hand, opposed passage in over 80 percent of the instances. Perhaps these numbers may be seen as affording some support to the small-business hypothesis.

Now having engaged in this exercise of witness counting, I have some doubt about its potential for yielding useful information. As I initially conceived the purpose of the exercise, it was to enable me to make statements of the form (should the numbers prove to justify them), "the small-business hypothesis is supported because such an extraordinarily large number of small-business witnesses were willing to incur the expenses associated with their appearance." But how does one decide, in this context, what an "extraordinarily large number" is? The possibility of making witness counts of hearings on more or less contemporaneous and "comparable" pieces of legislation occurred to me; and I made some efforts along those lines. But those efforts foundered on the extreme subjectivity involved in determining what was comparable legislation.

To be comparable, legislation must surely have its primary impact on the business community. Surely it should be applicable to all, or at least most, industries rather than being industry specific; for example, the Shipping Act of 1916 would fail on this ground to be comparable to the Clayton Act. But short of doing witness counts on hearings on all or a large sample of the very broad range of legislation falling within these criteria, I fail to see how one could be confident that he had cross-section data of any validity.

Neither does viewing the data from antitrust hearings as time series data seem to me to be very revealing. In the first place, the five legislative enactments dealt with here are very different in their character. The Sherman Act, portions of the Clayton Act, and the Antitrust Improvements Act seem to me, on their faces, to be much more nearly consistent with the public-interest hypothesis than is the Robinson-Patman Act, for example. Those differences, of course, are rooted in my own attitudes and experiences, and in those senses are subjective. Yet they seem to me clearly to dominate any systematic differences in witness patterns associated with the passage of time.

Finally, the process of identifying witnesses by category and of characterizing their testimony as pro or con is itself, I discovered, an uncertain and subjective enterprise. The testimony of many witnesses is so wildly extraneous to any issue that might fairly be thought under consideration that to count them in any category merely adds noise to the data. Many witnesses seem to be making a studied effort to find something good and something bad to say about the pending legislation, perhaps in an effort to enhance their credibility by demonstrating objectivity. Should such a witness nevertheless be counted as pro if it seems reasonably clear that the effect of his testimony, if any, is on balance favorable to passage? I decided so; another might not. I would find it difficult to persuade myself on another occasion that this exercise was worth replicating or extending.

Notes

1. William M. Landes and Richard A. Posner, "Adjudication as a Private Good," *Journal of Legal Studies* 8 (March 1979): 235, 267–285.

2. See Cities Supplement to the Statistical Abstracts, Cities over 25,000 Population, 1940.

3. See *County Data Book: A Supplement to the Statistical Abstracts of United States,* 1947.

4. The Data Users Services Division of the Census Bureau informed me that "most" of it is now available on tapes. (Telephone (301) 763-5042.)

5. The catalogue of materials available from IUCPSR is somewhat misleading in this respect. It indicates that the group has available magnetic tapes covering these volumes including "selected demographic and economic variables." The coverage is very selective indeed: it includes only population figures, voting data and some data on housing.

6. Individual votes on the two roll calls are set forth in *Congressional Quarterly Almanac* 32 (1976): 26h, 160h, roll-call votes No. 80 and No. 568.

Commentaries

2

Commentary:

Harlan M. Blake

Professor Baxter's paper provides its commentators with a wide and varied range of topics to choose among. This is in part because it has neither substantial empirical findings to present, as its author is first to tell us, nor a single model which is advanced as sufficiently powerful to explain the persistence of an effective political constituency for antitrust law over a period of ninety years or more.

What Professor Baxter hoped to have for us was apparently an empirical study of Congressional roll-call votes on antitrust legislation testing the hypothesis that a major political constituency of antitrust is made of small-business firms using their political advantage to impose legal disadvantages upon large firms in the industry in which they compete (his fourth, or "small-business," hypothesis). One of the many merits of the paper is that it provides us a detailed account of why the hoped-for results could not be attained from existing data, including a careful report on what data are available, machine readable and otherwise, and defining specific, more limited questions they might illuminate.

In addition to the small-business hypothesis, Professor Baxter presents three additional hypotheses (1) the consumer-protection (or public-interest) view, (2) self-interest of the antitrust bar, and (3) self-interest of antitrust bureaucrats—of which one feels he takes only the latter somewhat seriously. He also explores at length two additional possible means of testing the hypotheses—by analysis of antitrust litigation and by analysis of securities prices—but after detailed consideration of the possibilities largely rejects them as either unfeasible or unlikely to suitably discriminate among the hypotheses. En route, we get a quick but comprehensive tour of post-Director "Chicago-school" antitrust economics, Baxter version—presenting plenty of targets for commentary. Finally, we are given a study of classes of witnesses providing testimony at Congressional hearings on antitrust bills, modestly evaluated by the author as hardly worth the effort.

I will set forth briefly an alternative view of antitrust's political constituency to that reflected in Professor Baxter's hypotheses. I will then comment on one of his efforts at model-making which I found particularly striking, and on one rather arbitrarily selected feature of the article's antitrust analysis.

An Alternative View

Professor Baxter declares that the conventional hypothesis with respect to the political constituency for antitrust is that public-spirited legislators and judiciary enact and enforce antitrust laws "because they benefit all consumers in that their effect is to improve resource allocation. . . ." This makes Robert Bork and Richard Posner conventional and me unconventional. I have no objection to that view of matters, but there are some who might wonder if history is not being rewritten. Perhaps the more traditional view of antitrust is that it is a policy designed to preserve a competitive organization of industry in small units in spite of the possible cost of such a policy. This view sees competitive process and limiting market power an end in itself regardless of "efficiency" considerations.

As the centers of power grow larger the bureaucracies, governmental or corporate, which wield that power apparently grow at a greater than arithmetic rate and take their toll in impeding more productive economic activity. Many students of American political history regard this heritage of resistance to concentration of power as one of our major national treasures, and it will not do to demean it by phrases like Professor Baxter's "Populist posturings."

Professor Baxter doubts that so generalized a political force as consumer welfare (or presumably any of the social values described by other observers) can be effective in providing support for antitrust, since candidates for public office, like radio broadcasters, will not find it worthwhile to differentiate their product to appeal to the relatively small part of the electorate (or market) which sees antitrust as a salient issue.

Here I think Professor Baxter's political history fails him. Legislation reflecting fundamental public policy, not so very differently from the federal Constitution itself, does not require continuous white-heat political priority at the top of the agenda of public concerns. Our substantive antitrust laws are largely found in four pieces of legislation. In the major political campaigns immediately preceding each of them—in 1888, prior to the Sherman Act; in 1912, prior to the Clayton and Federal Trade Commission Acts; and to a lesser degree in 1948, prior to the Celler-Kefauver Act—antitrust issues to which those laws were a response *had* risen to a high level of political urgency.

In the long intervening spans between landmark legislative efforts, the special interest groups to which Professor Baxter accords greater political potency, are frequently effectively at work, seeking and sometimes securing special antitrust exemptions or reduced appropriations or other constraints on enforcement. The list of such special interest statutes is a fairly long one, affecting agriculture, banking, wholesale and retail distribution, exports, newspaper publishing among others.

But in these special confrontations, as well as in efforts to secure more modest legislation strengthening penalties and enforcement procedures, for example, another constituency—the enforcement bureaucracy in the Antitrust Division and Federal Trade Commission—are often adequate to win the day with only limited specific input from the general public. As recognized in Professor Baxter's fourth hypothesis, antitrust enforcement has of course become institutionalized and the institution defends its raison d'être. However, I would attribute the continuing zeal of the enforcement agencies not entirely to a desire for "the expansion of their own power and their own budgets," as Professor Baxter seems to do, but also to a rather commonly shared human belief that what one elects to devote one's life to is worth doing.

In sum, I think Professor Baxter's approach is defective, first, in its assumption that the only objective of the antitrust laws is "economic efficiency," whatever that concept means as transferred from the context of Coasian theory to that of public policy; and second, in seeking to fit analysis of political constituencies into the inadequate and Procrustean bed of exclusively microeconomic assumption about human motivation. Basic values and ideas have political consequences, and to fail to deal with all of them is likely to limit the validity and usefulness of research.

Rivalry among Firms

I find puzzling one feature of Professor Baxter's interesting model seeking to explain why large firms represent a rivalrous threat to small firms that other small firms do not. Absent such an explanation, he perceives that he must abandon or modify his hypothesis that antitrust finds a major constituency in small firms seeking to handicap large firms (in the same industry). If he were less of a "purist" he would be willing to rely upon what most small businessmen doubtless believe to be the case—that a large rival can and may employ competitive strategies unavailable to small firms that will disadvantage him. Especially in the context of political motivation, that would seem to be a plausible assumption. But Professor Baxter subscribes rigorously to the postulate that no substantial group long continues to act— even in political matters—on a mistaken factual assumption about its own economic self-interest, and since Professor Baxter believes such an assumption—that larger firms are more dangerous competitors—to be mistaken, a more elegant solution must be found. His suggestion is that small businesses typically enjoy a limited locational advantage over distant competitors which is gradually eroded away by economies of scale or new technology available to large but not small competitors. Thus larger firms *do* represent a greater competitive threat, and it is presumably "efficient" that they do so. But it is also rational that small business seek to impose legal burdens upon them.

My problem is why Professor Baxter limits his hypothesis to rivalries between small businesses and larger potential competitors in the same product market. Surely another important class of antitrust customer is small business which feels threatened by larger potential competitors in nearby product markets, whose efficiency or competitive advantages, should there be entry, would rapidly eliminate any margin of advantage currently enjoyed by the smaller firms. (One group that readily comes to mind is the computer industry's suppliers of peripheral equipment, software, and data processing service.) Would the model not be more elegant if it were not limited to the special case of temporary spatial isolation but extended to include temporary product isolation more likely to be ended by product-extension moves by larger firms? Analytically the cases seem to be indistinguishable, although in historical terms Professor Baxter may be justified in limiting his interest to the spatial case.

Methodology

Professor Baxter frequently makes predictions about the results of putative empirical work—with respect to stock market prices, for example—which he would expect in support of one or another hypothesis, on the basis of assumptions about effects of antitrust rules, which have more relevance to a static competitive model than to the dynamics of specific industry situations. I wonder if this is not poor methodology in that it could lead to embracing or rejecting the wrong research undertaking.

One of many such instances is with respect to the *Fortner* type tie-in, which he asserts to be clearly allocatively efficient. Kenneth Dam's early analysis of the facts of the *Fortner* case made it clear that the easy credit terms for Fortner were a form of localized price-cutting which, absent predatory circumstances, he believed to be in the best interest of consumers. I remain doubtful of this point.

But for the credit arrangement under litigation, U.S. Steel's prefabricated housing unit would have been faced with two alternatives—either to reduce its apparently excessive prices across the board, or to commit resources to a longer-range attempt to improve the quality of its apparently somewhat substandard product. The credit "tie" apparently made it possible for U.S. Steel to avoid these alternatives by fine-tuning its sales terms to individual situations—in other words, by engaging in nonsystematic price discrimination among its various customers. If the industry were one characterized by oligopoly price and quality behavior, is it not possible that the availability of the tie would serve to protect these rigidities from the erosive force of direct price concessions or competition through investment in improving quality? And if the firm's single-product competitors have no comparable access to large tax-privileged retained earnings, can we be sure that the eventual equilibrium posture of the industry will be the optimum for consumers? May not producers of better or less expensive products be "unfairly" eliminated? Perhaps competitors can "go and do likewise" by becoming part of an equivalent conglomerate enterprise, as my colleague Jones suggests, but that does not seem to me to be the best result in terms either of economic efficiency, whatever that means, or other antitrust values.

This by no means exhausts my repertory of concern about the version of antitrust economics assumed in Professor Baxter's paper, but that is a larger subject matter than can be dealt with here.

3

Commentary:

Yale Brozen

Professor Baxter's paper explores some territory which has intrigued many of us in the industrial organization field. I and others have attempted some guesses about the features that might be found in this landscape, but they have been based on little evidence other than such coincidences as a 25 percent fall in prices from 1882 to 1890, complaints about predatory pricing and the enactment of the Sherman Act in 1890. A similar 25 percent fall in prices from 1929 to 1933 and complaints about excessive competition was followed by a virtual suspension of the antitrust laws. It would seem that passage and suspension of antitrust measures serve as symbolic acts indicating concern about a problem such as deflation (or inflation).[1]

Baxter presents alternative hypotheses concerning the effects of antitrust and the alternative or several interests which may be served. Presumably, the constituency or constituencies of antitrust are to be found by determining whose interests are benefited. The interests could be (1) the public interest (by enhancing efficiency and producing more for consumers), (2) small businesses (by protecting companies from the competition of more efficient, larger firms or from the competition of cheating members of a cartel), (3) bureaucrats who want larger empires over which to preside and promotions, or (4) lawyers who win large fees by private enforcement of antitrust laws (which may or may not serve the public interest since some antitrust doctrines promote competition and efficiency while others hinder competition and efficiency). Inasmuch as the promotion of the interest of one group may also provide benefits to others, some of Baxter's proposed means of finding whose interests are served or whose "ox is gored" will not clearly distinguish among the various potential constituencies. Perhaps more than one is served by antitrust and more than one supports antitrust along with ideologues who oppose big business, all business, or who simply favor the dispersion of power, or at least the power outside the hands of those who compose the apparatus of the state.

Some Anecdotal Evidence

Some anecdotal evidence, for whatever it is worth, seems to support one of Professor Baxter's hypotheses: antitrust is intended to provide protection for small business and small business supports antitrust to obtain such protection. One such bit of evidence is provided by events preceding the bringing of an antitrust case against the Great Atlantic & Pacific Company (A & P). The news that antitrust indictment would be sought against the Great Atlantic & Pacific Company (A & P) was disclosed by the Department of Justice at a convention of wholesale grocers. The National Association of Retail Grocers had petitioned earlier for an investigation of A & P.[2]

When Senator Kefauver and his committee were investigating the pricing of pharmaceuticals, the major manufacturers of drugs were drawn and quartered to the great delight of the mob with hardly a congressional murmur of dissent. The investigation paraded under the banner of consumer interests. When it was suggested to Senator Kefauver that the retailing of pharmaceuticals be investigated since manufacturers received only 48 percent of the retail price, that investigation was killed within 48 hours after the idea was broached.

Little Utah Pie, with 64 percent of the Salt Lake City market for frozen berry pies, was awarded a remand by the Supreme Court to find damages caused by big Carnation, Pet, and Continental who dared compete with it.[3] I have been told that the Supreme Court has been known to read the election returns and also is aware of congressional sentiments with respect to small business.

There are many pieces of evidence that pro-small-business and anti-big-business sentiment is strong at both the congressional and state legislature levels—sentiment which is protectionist in character. The federal laws forbidding interstate branching by banks and state laws restricting intrastate branching is one such piece. The state laws prohibiting the importation of "foreign" meat from other states, ruled unconstitutional by the courts, were aimed at the big packers and to protect local butchers and local livestock growers and feeders. The provisions of the federal Dealer-Day-in-Court Act and the state restrictions on auto company franchising of additional dealers in Massachusetts, California, Texas, and eleven other states is another bit of evidence. Maryland's, and thirty other states', prohibition of refiner operation of filling stations is in the same genre. The federal corporate earnings tax rates, which have become progressive, is still another. Add to this the subsidies provided for loans to small business. Also, the favorable quotas given to small oil refiners under the old mandatory oil import quota program,[4] the favorable entitlement grants to small refiners with under 10,000 barrels a day capacity in the current control program (which has amounted to a $750,000,000 a year susidy to 41 "ma-and-pa" refiners), and the retention of depletion allowances for small producers while repealing them for large producers support this thesis.[5]

But the pro-small-business sentiment does not run uniformly throughout the legislative and antitrust establishment. Sometimes different parts of the governmental establishment go in opposite directions. When the Federal Trade Commission (FTC) attacked the seven major soft drink concentrate producers for granting exclusive territories to their bottlers, their complaints to Congress fell on deaf ears. After the concentrate producers informed their franchisees at a bottler's convention that their exclusive territories might be abolished, 106 bills legalizing exclusive territories hit the congressional hopper. But no bill has yet been passed and the FTC continues to persist in its efforts to remove territorial protection for small bottlers. Inasmuch as removal of such protection would serve neither small business nor consumers, does this mean that bureaucrats use antitrust to seek more power?

Even within the same agency, disparate behavior is found. When the Federal Paper Board Company, which was number three in glass tableware with 11 percent of the market, accepted the offer of $40 million for its Federal Glass division from Lancaster, which was number seven in the industry with 7 percent of the market, Anchor-Hocking, the number one firm in the industry, complained to the FTC. The combined sales of Federal and Lancaster were less than Libbey's, the number two firm, and far less than those of Anchor-Hocking.[6] Yet, the FTC responded to Anchor's objections to Lancaster's acquisition of Federal by obtaining an injunction to halt the sale and instituting a complaint against the proposed acquisition. The fact that Anchor objected should have been grounds for allowing the acquisition since the objection demonstrated that it was procompetitive.

At the same time that the acquisition negotiations between Lancaster and Federal were collapsing because of the delays by and objections of the FTC, Anchor was in process of acquiring Brockway Glass's division which produced about 9 percent of the tableware sold in the United States. The FTC raised no barrier to the acquisition of a company very nearly the same size as Federal by the number one firm in the industry although it objected to the number seven firm's acquisition of Federal. It seems to have favored the largest firm in the industry over a much smaller firm for no discernable reason. Also, the business done by Federal has largely gone to the leading two firms since Federal has been liquidated, failing the sale of the business to Lancaster.

The anecdotal evidence is not only confusing; it is also notorious for illustrating an observer's prejudices which seem to induce selective perception. Someone unfriendly to Professor Baxter's hypothesis might point not only to the Federal Glass episode at the FTC but also to the exemptions from the antitrust laws won in Congress by big railroads in the Reed-Bulwinkle Act and by the big insurance companies in the McCarran Act (although the McCarran Act exempted small as well as large firms). Of course, balancing this are the exemptions won by farmers in the Capper-Volstead Act, by the labor unions in the Clayton Act, and by the professions in times past. Also, the Robinson-Patman, McGuire, and Miller-

Tydings Acts were the result of the anti-big-chain-store sentiments of small retailers.[7] There is, in recent years, some erosion of these exemptions in the courts and outright repeal of the McGuire Act. I take these to be an outgrowth of anti-inflation sentiments more broadly appealing than pro-small-business sentiments.

Evidence from Securities Markets

Baxter proposes cosmic research rather than countervailing lists of anecdotes. The use of information from securities markets, which can produce generalizations with less sample bias, is suggested in his paper. His list of needed research endeavors is a rich mine of dissertation suggestions into which doctoral students searching for thesis topics would be well-advised to delve. As a matter of fact, he has "anticipated" three dissertations—one at the University of Chicago completed by James C. Ellert in 1975, one at the University of Minnesota also completed in 1975, and one now being completed at the University of California, Los Angeles, by Robert Stillman.[8]

The Minnesota dissertation by Malcolm Burns deals with the Section 2 cases on which Professor Baxter asked for the light that can be shed by securities markets. Burns finds that "Statistical test of the [security] price changes accompanying important developments in the litigation show rather strongly that investors did not expect dissolution [of Standard Oil, American Tobacco, and American Snuff] to alter the performance of the snuff, tobacco, and petroleum industries." He concludes that either "these industries were essentially competitive prior to 1912" or there was no competition between successor companies. Stockholders of the three combinations were not hurt provided that they did not sell after news of the complaints in 1907 or after the news of the Supreme Court's American Tobacco decision on 29 May 1911. Those who had their securities from precomplaint days to mid-1912 suffered no loss (and may have gained in the tobacco and petroleum dissolutions).[9] There would be no reason for the investors who held their securities or for those whose firms might be subjected to similar dissolution actions to be opponents of the antitrust laws.

According to Baxter, "the securities price history of the [Section 2] monopoly and its surviving parts would not help us to distinguish among the several hypotheses. All of the hypotheses would predict that the post-litigation securities value of the monopoly enterprise would fall . . . [whether] the dismemberment is viewed as a sideshow, incidental to the enrichment of the antitrust bar, or the expansion of the public sector, or as an anticompetitive device to improve the fortune of small peripheral competitors [or as an end to exploitive monopoly]." Since the securities prices in the three dismemberments examined by Burns were no lower in the post-decree period than in the precomplaint period relative to the market, does that mean that all the hypotheses are wrong? Should we seek alternative hypotheses to test? Of course, to complete Baxter's proposed test, the behavior of the securities of competitors has yet to be examined.

As for the *Shoe Machinery* case which Baxter suggests we examine, I have no securities data at the moment. Baxter suggests that the public-interest hypothesis would be substantiated if the value of United Shoe Machinery securities and those of established peripheral firms both fall (and those of firms at which predation was directed rise). The small-business hypothesis would be substantiated if all competitor and peripheral firms rise and United falls.

My own bet as to what will be found when we examine security prices of shoe machinery companies and of major shoe manufacturers is that they *all* rose and that those of small shoe manufacturers fell. My expectation will not be borne out if treble damages assessed are important to United and to shoe manufacturers. Unfortunately for the test, I expect that this was the case although I have no estimate at hand of these. Also, this is a period of rising shoe imports (which would depress the security prices of United and of *all* shoe manufacturers to the extent that it was not fully anticipated).

The reason for my expectation is the anticompetitive effect in the shoe industry of the Wyzanski decree. Wyzanski's decree eliminated the ten-year minimum term for leases and the provision of "free" repair service. I would expect the annual rentals on short term leases to be higher than on long term leases. Also, the rentals in "new" leases must have been higher than on the old leases which were canceled since inflation had occurred after the old leases were written, in many cases. In addition, the lack of a priority use clause, which was banned by the decree, led United to set higher minimum monthly rentals (and lower royalties). The use of high minimum monthly rentals more than offset potential lower royalties.[10] Small shoe manufacturers would lose because of the higher rentals for shorter term leases and the replacement of high royalties by high minimum rentals. My guess is that it was large manufacturers who took most of the machines purchased. They were in a position to take the risk that a line of shoes might not sell well since other lines that do sell well could be produced on otherwise idle machines.[11] Also, with enough machines, large manufacturers could provide their own repair service. It was they who must have been the main beneificiaries of the shoe machinery decree. Their securities should rise if the changes to ownership and self-repair of machines plus the decreased competition from small manufacturers had a more than *de minimus* effect. All this is speculation. Yet these types of questions should be answered. The shoe machinery case is worth a more sophisticated examination than that provided by Kaysen and an after-the-fact examination of the effect of the decree.

Baxter turns next to cases involving horizontal price-fixing, telling us that "share prices should drop as a result of enforcement; and this is true whether the asserted behavior is allocatively inefficient, as minimum price fixing almost inevitably is, or whether the behavior is efficient, as basing point pricing or the exchange of data among competitors might well be."

James Ellert has examined share price behavior in 202 conspiracy cases brought by the Federal Trade Commission (FTC) and 566 cases brought by the Department of Justice. In the FTC cases, abnormal returns are "not significantly different from zero for . . . defendants before complaints, at the announcement of formal investigations, during litigation or after litigation."[12] (See table 3-1). He suggests that the FTC is simply used by unsuccessful competitors as an instrument for harassing successful competitors. "Over the 100 months leading to complaints, FTC conspiracy respondents had an ACCR of 10.4 percent. This compares to 2.7 percent for defendants in similar actions brought by the Justice Department."[13] Should this be regarded as substantiating Baxter's small business protection hypothesis? Ellert's respondents are NYSE listed firms which generally are larger firms while complainants are probably smaller firms.

The ACCR is a nonsignificant 2.7 percent for defendants in Justice Department conspiracy cases over the 100 months preceding a complaint (see table 3-1) and the average monthly raw portfolio residual is slightly negative. "It is unlikely that a typical pricing agreement would persist undetected over such a long period. The data do not suggest that shareholders benefited from these conspiracies."[14] Nor did they lose significantly when the conspiracies were dissolved, which we would expect since the conspiracies had no benefit (unless it can be argued that the conspirators who showed no abnormal gains from conspiracy would have suffered abnormal losses but for the conspiracy[15]). But they do lose later from the treble damage actions brought despite the fact that buyers were not damaged. Treble damages appear to be windfall gains to private plaintiffs.

Unfortunately, Ellert lumped all tie-in cases with several other "abuses" such as predatory pricing and patent misuse. His work does not shed any light on these cases to which Baxter devotes extensive, and illuminating discussion.

Ellert also lumps all *Robinson-Patman* cases together without distinguishing between primary-line and other cases. In his 184 FTC price discrimination cases, security prices of offending sellers do not fall despite Baxter's contrary expectations. There is no abnormal loss before a case is brought, none at the time of complaint, none during litigation, and none after settlement (see table 3-1).

As for the merger cases, what appears to be most notable about them is that cases are brought against acquiring firms with the most efficient managements who are likely to make the most efficient use of acquired assets. The 279 firms against which proceedings were brought earned abnormal returns of 26 percent in the 100 months *before* acquisition while the 493 acquiring firms not indicted earned abnormal returns of only 18 percent before making an acquisition. In both instances, most of the abnormal return had been earned in the period preceding the four years before the acquisition so that it was not the prospect of the acquisition and "capitalization of monopoly rents" that generated the premerger abnormal gains.[16]

The selection of firms ordered to divest among those against whom cases were brought was even more perverse. The 123 defendants ordered to divest acquired assets provided abnormal returns of 30.8 percent to their stockholders in the 100 months prior to acquisition. The less effective managements whose stock provided only 11.9 percent abnormal returns were allowed to keep their acquired assets.[17]

The behavior of security values of defendants in merger cases following settlement provides further confirmation of the nonmonopoly motive for merger. The loss of stockholder wealth whether or not ordered to divest acquired assets was zero in the 48 months following settlement. There was a loss of 1.8 percent at the time complaints were brought, but this is attributable to the cost of defense (including diversion of executive attention and time and the effects of uncertainty on decision making).

Baxter suggests examining the impact of horizontal mergers on the wealth of stockholders in rival concerns. If horizontal mergers improve efficiency and benefit consumers, the value of competitors' assets should fall. If increased market shares in the hands of acquiring firms enables them to influence output and prices in ways adverse to consumers (Baxter's public-interest hypothesis)—holding a price umbrella, for example—then the wealth of the owners of competing firms can be expected to increase. With the dissolution of horizontal mergers, opposite effects would follow.

Robert Stillman, in his dissertation at UCLA, investigated the effects of horizontal mergers and of dissolutions of horizontal mergers using this methodology. The central question that he asked was, "Do the antitrust enforcers tend to challenge price-increasing mergers?[18] He concluded that, "The evidence is that there has been no such tendency." Perhaps this follows from the fact that "the data on rivals' abnormal stock returns indicate that the proportion" of wealth increases for firms competing with merged firms does not appear any different than the proportion to be expected if there had been no mergers to benefit or hurt them. But it might have been expected that the antitrust authorities would challenge selected mergers, that is, those which would produce some market impact. Evidently, antitrusters did no better than challenge a random selection of mergers in their dissolution complaints.

These data assembled by Stillman show neither favorable nor adverse effects on rivals of merged firms. The implication follows that horizontal

Table 3–1
Analysis of Two-factor Market Model Residuals in Selected Periods Surrounding Antitrust Events—Summary Results

	Sample Size	K = -100 L = MC - 1			K = MC L = MC			K = MC L = MS			K = 1 L = 48		
		ACCR	t	% CCR > 0.0	ACCR	t	% CCR > 0.0	ACCR	t	% CCR > 0.0	ACCR	t	% CCR > 0.0
Total Sample	1466	.063	1.35	.51	-.010	-4.22	.46*	-.017	-0.35	.47*	-.023	-0.98	.47
Dismissal	388	.055	1.57	.51*	-.013	-3.13	.43*	-.033	-0.47	.46	.018	-0.06	.55
Guilty	389	.131	2.34	.58*	-.007	-1.43	.46	-.012	-0.05	.47	.006	-0.46	.48
Consent decree	471	.034	0.33	.49	-.013	-3.26	.39*	-.026	-0.97	.45*	-.032	-0.83	.47
Nolo contendere	218	.023	-0.07	.45	-.008	-0.91	.42*	.021	1.01	.58	-.132	-2.70	.37*
Merger	216	.172	2.52	.57*	-.019	-3.86	.38*	-.033	-1.13	.41*	-.020	-0.69	.46
Horizontal conspiracy	768	.047	0.70	.52	-.010	-2.60	.42*	-.025	-0.13	.48	-.038	-1.05	.46
Abuse	84	-.007	0.26	.50	-.016	-3.49	.33*	.073	1.66	.50	-.022	-0.17	.48
Price discrimination	184	-.015	-0.53	.44	-.006	-0.57	.47	.015	0.79	.45	.008	0.40	.50
Deceptive practices	214	.107	1.65	.51	-.006	-0.44	.46	-.038	-1.09	.42*	.005	-0.42	.50
Appealed cases	203	.218	3.26	.67*	-.014	-0.84	.46	-.036	-0.28	.43*	.000	-0.18	.45
Merger/divestiture	115	.242	3.51	.59*	-.018	-3.20	.41*	-.042	-0.78	.43	-.016	-0.53	.47
Justice Department	753	.050	0.92	.51	-.016	-4.24	.38*	-.019	-0.24	.48	-.056	-1.75	.45*
Dismissal	185	.062	1.33	.55*	-.018	-2.40	.35*	-.035	-0.37	.46	.002	-0.29	.52
Guilty	93	.158	1.38	.65*	-.017	-1.88	.43	-.019	0.35	.47	.009	0.11	.46
Consent decree	257	.025	0.38	.47	-.020	-3.91	.36*	-.041	-0.78	.46	-.051	-1.20	.46
Nolo contendere	218	.023	-0.07	.45	-.008	-0.91	.42*	.021	1.01	.51	-.132	-2.70	.37*

Merger	128	.161	2.02	.55	−.026	−3.94	.33*	−.015	−0.27	.49	.004	0.25	.49
Horizontal conspiracy	566	.027	0.30	.50	−.012	−3.01	.40*	−.029	−0.45	.47	−.067	−1.98	.44*
Abuse	59	.024	0.94	.52	−.023	−2.91	.27*	.076	1.53	.53	−.046	−0.24	.46
Criminal suits	352	.058	0.71	.52	−.009	−1.65	.42*	−.031*	−1.13	.45	−.062	−1.45	.43*
Civil suits	401	.043	0.73	.50*	−.022	−4.70	.35*	−.008	−0.35	.49	−.049	−1.10	.46
Followed by private suit	85	.189	2.03	.62	−.019	−2.10	.33*	.046	1.04	.54	−.162	−2.33	.29*
Federal Trade Commission	713	.078	1.99	.52	−.005	−1.26	.47	−.016	−0.33	.46*	.011	−0.05	.50
Dismissal	203	.049	1.41	.47*	−.007	−1.67	.50	−.033	−0.43	.46	.032	0.45	.58
Cease and desist order	296	.123	2.46	.56*	−.003	−0.56	.47*	−.010	0.00	.47	.005	−0.40	.47
Consent decree	214	.045	0.18	.50	−.004	−0.75	.43*	−.009	−0.51	.43	−.001	−0.44	.48
Merger	88	.189	2.03	.59*	−.009	−1.42	.44	−.059	−1.78	.42	−.049	−0.91	.43
Horizontal conspiracy	202	.104	1.14	.58*	−.003	−0.04	.48	−.013	0.39	.52	.039	0.99	.54
Abuse	25	−.082	−0.31	.45	.001	−1.18	.48	.087	−0.15	.52	.032	0.51	.53
Price discrimination	184	−.015	−0.53	.44	−.006	−0.57	.47	.015	0.79	.45	.008	0.40	.50
Deceptive practices	214	.107	1.68	.51	−.006	−0.44	.46	−.038	−1.09	.41*	.005	−0.42	.50

Source: James C. Ellert, *Antitrust Enforcement and the Behavior of Stock Prices* (1975):80. Reprinted with permission.

*$X^2 > 3.84$; Probability ($X^2 > 3.84$/Population percentage $= .50$) $= .05$ for 1 degree of freedom.

mergers had neither the effect of facilitating tacit or explicit collusion nor of improving efficiency. Why, then, did they take place? There seems to be no need to answer that question in connection with any attempt to discriminate among Baxter's hypotheses concerning the political constituency of antitrust, but it may be added to the agenda for future research.[19] The answer could be helpful in focusing antitrust activities on targets which would better serve the public interest than spending our resources on attacking a Brown-Kinney merger creating a firm with a 5-percent market share or a Vons-Shopping Bag merger creating a 8.9-percent firm in a hotly competitive local market.

Notes

1. The inflation of the past decade has been met with a flurry of amendments which have increased antitrust penalties and eased the task of bringing antitrust complaints.

2. Morris Adelman, *A & P: A Study in Price-Cost Behavior and Public Policy* (1959), p. 328.

3. See Ward Bowman, "Restraint of Trade by the Supreme Court: The Utah Pie Case," *Yale Law Journal* 77(1968):70, reprinted in Y. Brozen, *The Competitive Economy: Selected Readings* (1975):447.

4. George J. Stigler, "The Theory of Economic Regulation," *Bell Journal of Economics and Management Science* 2(1971):7.

5. For an analysis of the effects of the division of the political market into geographical areas, see W. Mark Crain, "On the Structure and Stability of Political Markets," *Journal of Political Economy* 85(1977):829.

6. A.F. Ehrbar, "The Needless Death of Federal Glass," *Fortune* (July 2, 1979):59.

7. All states passed a chain-store tax prior to 1936. Many were invalidated but eleven still had them in 1936. Adelman, p. 53.

8. Another dissertation also performs some of the tests suggested by Professor Baxter, but its samples are small and its analysis of security price reactions to vertical rearrangements is confined to a single industry. D.R. Kummer, "Stock Price Reaction to Announcements of Forced Divestitures," *Journal of Midwest Finance Association* 5(1976):99.

9. Malcolm R. Burns, "The Competitive Effects of Trust-Busting: A Portfolio Analysis," *Journal of Political Economy* 85(1977):717.

10. Carl Kaysen, *United States* v. *United Shoe Machinery Corporation* (1956):324–325.

11. Wesley J. Liebeler, "Market Power and Competitive Superiority in Concentrated Industries," *UCLA Law Review* 25(August 1978):1231–1300.

12. James C. Ellert, *Antitrust Enforcement and the Behavior of Stock Prices* (1975):80.

13. ACCR is the average company cumulative residual "formed by cumulating abnormal residuals across time for individual securities and then averaging across companies." Ibid., p. 56.

14. Ibid., p. 123.

15. There may be some grounds for this argument. Peter Asch and J.J. Seneca, "Is Collusion Profitable?" *Review of Economics and Statistics* 58(1976):1.

16. James C. Ellert, "Mergers, Antitrust Law Enforcement and Stockholder Returns," *Journal of Finance* 31(1976):727.

17. Ibid., p. 721.

18. Robert Stillman, *Examining the Antitrust Case Against Horizontal Mergers* (1979).

19. One possible answer is that horizontal mergers do result in efficiency gains but rivals do not suffer because the efficiency gains are not passed on to buyers. If there are efficiency gains, and no misallocation of resources as a consequence of price-raising effects, then there is a clear social gain. Resources are released to add to the economy's total output— resources which otherwise would have been concerned in inefficient production. There is, then, a clear social loss from the harsh application of the Celler-Kefauver Amendment.

A sample of postwar horizontal mergers too small to yield clearly significant data, analyzed by Paul Asquith in some unpublished work, points in this direction. Acquired firms showed no abnormal losses in the four years prior to acquisition, and significant abnormal market gains shortly before and at the announcement of the proposed merger. Acquiring firms showed normal returns at the time of announcement and in the year following the horizontal merger despite the payment of substantial premiums. Normal returns could have been earned in these circumstances (accepting Stillwell's finding of no more than the usual proportion of abnormal gainers among rivals) only if efficiency was improved sufficiently to yield a return on the premiums.

4

Commentary:

Kenneth W. Dam

Rather than providing a critique of what Baxter says in his paper, I should like to reflect upon the task that Baxter set for himself and then relate that task to the subject of this seminar—The Political Economy of Antitrust.

At the outset let me give a short and tendentious summary of Baxter's paper. He states that he set out originally to "attempt to identify the political constituency for the passage and enforcement of the antitrust laws of the United States." He posits four possible constituencies and asks which *one* is *the* constituency. The four are: first, consumers ("public-spirited legislators pass these laws and the public-spirited judiciary enforces them because they benefit all consumers. . . ."); the second possible constituency is the private bar; the third, public officials ("who view antitrust as a relatively low cost vehicle for the expansion of their own power and their own benefit"); and the fourth is small business (or at least particular small firms). Baxter then reviews the evidence that could be used to support each of these four hypotheses and finds, with very limited exceptions, that the requisite data do not exist, or in some instances exist in principle but would be too expensive to reduce to a form that would lend itself to statistical analysis. In still other instances the data would be ambiguous even if they did exist.

Using conventional criteria, Baxter's paper is, of course, a failure. He does not even test a hypothesis, much less does so successfully. But his paper is nonetheless interesting, not so much for what he tells us about the data (or lack thereof) but for what he says about the substantive antitrust rules in tracing their implications for political support, securities prices, and the like. His paper demonstrates the formidable power of strictly abstract reasoning in helping us to understand the implications of substantive antitrust rules.

What we observe in Baxter's paper is one result of the current intellectual imperialism of high-powered economists who (1) believe that economics can be used to uncover nearly all knowledge worth having about our social and political institutions; and (2) profess that there is little worth knowing about those institutions that cannot be expressed in quantitative terms. In this imperialist war, economics is their strategy and regressions their preferred weapons.

Obviously it is important to the development of economics as a social science to improve the ability of economists to use quantitative methods. But I do not accept the implicit premise that all useful hypotheses must be not only testable but also tested by quantitative methods. Consequently, I am not left with the sense of despair communicated by the Baxter paper as a result of its data failure.

Certainly in the study of substantive antitrust rules, what we have learned in what I shall call the "Director revolution" (by which I mean the work that derives from Aaron Director's thoughts) can be attributed almost solely to abstract reasoning. The empirical work in that revolution has been quite modest. It has consisted largely of looking at judicial opinions, not for empirical verification, but rather for raw material. And what empirical work has been done, and by far the most valuable, has consisted of analyzing trial records and specific factual material related to decided cases. (Most of that work has been published over the years in the *Journal of Law and Economics*.) That work certainly does not meet the quantitative standards to which Baxter aspires and is in no sense systematic.

At this point most of my readers will be inclined to say, "All right, Dam, what do you suggest we do?" I would be the first to admit that my suggestions are exceedingly modest.

Nevertheless, a few directions for new work can be suggested. An obvious first step in laying out a research agenda is the posing of interesting questions. The question posed by Baxter does not strike me as particularly interesting. It seems obvious to me that all four of Baxter's constituencies exist and have had a role in antitrust legislation and enforcement. The question is therefore not which one is the right one, but rather how the coalitions among these four constituencies are formed and how those coalitions operate and maintain themselves over time. Even if constituencies do not change, coalitions must constantly be renegotiated as the legislative agenda changes. And in the struggle for political power in the Congress, individual legislators specialize in particular issues and thereby become independent actors separate and apart from constituencies in their districts or states.

Nor is the constituency question precisely posed. Baxter does not define a constituency, but it is evident from remarks scattered through the paper that he has several, not always consistent, definitions in mind. With respect to antitrust legislation, he sometimes appears to define the constituency as those who were responsible for enacting the legislation. Yet at other times he clearly envisions those who benefit from the legislation. These may not always be the same set, although obviously there will normally be considerable overlap. They may be different sets, not solely because of ignorance but also because, for example, one may rationally support antitrust legislation as a long-run political alternative to state ownership or to pervasive regulation of industry.

Competing definitions of constituency may easily be posed. In enforcement matters one may define it as those to whom the relevant bureaucrats are accountable. A government antitrust official may be accountable, for example, to his colleagues in the legal profession (say, in the Washington antitrust bar) in the sense that a failure to maintain conventional legal standards may injure his career. Hence, this constituency may play a crucial role in influencing the style and even the content of enforcement.

I raise these questions not to quibble but rather to suggest that in discussing the Political Economy of Antitrust, there are a great many questions to be investigated. Even if we are dealing with constituency questions, for example, it is not clear to me that historical analysis cannot shed light on the sources of support for antitrust legislation by more direct methods. For example, using roll-call analysis not merely of antitrust bill roll calls but also of roll calls on other legislation where the winners and losers are more clearly defined, one may come better to understand the sources of support for antitrust legislation.

More generally, in discussing how one can learn something about the political economy of antitrust, it is important to ask why we want to investigate that subject. In that light, Baxter's question about which is *the* constituency strikes me as a question driven more by methodological preconceptions about what is academically respectable than by the inherent interest of the question. Consider the following objectives of any inquiry into the political economy of antitrust. We may want to be able to predict what kinds of legislation will be proposed, what kinds will be enacted and what kinds will be enforced vigorously (and by the FTC, the Antitrust Division, and private plaintiffs, respectively). We may be interested as citizens in affecting the outcomes of legislative deliberations and enforcement actions and therefore seek to understand the process in order to be able to influence the outcomes. We may want to reform the process itself. Finally, we may simply be driven by a burning curiosity about how the antitrust legislative and enforcement processes function in actual practice.

These interests, which are surely as honorable as "scientific" interests, may lead us to acquire many different kinds of factual information, some quantitative and some institutional. In addition to studying the formation and behavior of legislative coalitions, we may want to investigate funding levels over time for the FTC and the Antitrust Division, staffing levels for the Senate Antitrust Subcommittee, career paths for enforcement officials, procedural rules applied in private antitrust litigation (class action, discovery, litigation cost, and similar rules), the strategy and tactics of Senator Kennedy in using proposals for conglomerate merger and oil merger legislation to run for president, and a variety of other matters determining what has happened and is happening in the antitrust world.

One can think of analogies. Let us consider one from the judicial system. The Supreme Court is an important institution in society and many of us know a great deal about it as a result of studying judicial opinions, biographies, extrajudicial writings and utterances of the justices, caseload sta-

tistics, and the like. If we were to ask a Baxter-type question about the constituencies of the Supreme Court and then attempt to do regression analysis
to answer that question, we would probably not add much that was useful
to our knowledge (though I would be the last to say that that question
should not be studied if someone believes he can make any progress on it).

A small step in the direction that I am suggesting has been taken in
Suzanne Weaver's book on *The Decision to Prosecute.*[1] This book provides
a close look at the role of staff attorneys and their various superiors in the
Antitrust Division in decisions on choice of cases. Although her work suf-
fers from an evident lack of understanding of the substantive law and from
an unrelenting focus on only one aspect of the enforcement process (as well
as an exclusive reliance on interviews and an inability to obtain systematic
access to internal Antitrust Division documents), her work is enormously
illuminating for anyone who has not served in an enforcement agency. It
illustrates, for example, the great importance to prosecutorial decisions of
career paths, the advocacy (as opposed to the inquisitorial) process, and the
entrenched legal ethic that laws on the books should be enforced. Most of
us take these characteristics of enforcement more or less for granted, but we
find such information and insights difficult to integrate with other information and use in any systematic fashion. Perhaps that is only because we have
so few studies like Weaver's that we are seldom forced to think seriously
and persistently about how the antitrust laws function in practice.

Let us recognize that the political economy of antitrust is, particularly
on the enforcement as opposed to the legislation side, concerned with how
government decisions are made. That is a study area that we should con-
front directly, rather than approach solely as a question of economics. Let
me suggest an analogy from another field—strategic studies.

Academic work in the field of strategic studies was, even a decade ago,
limited largely to writings on strategic doctrine. Commentators posed a
series of questions about how the two major superpowers would react to
each other under various scenarios. Out of that doctrinal writing came a
series of propositions, notably MAD (mutual assured destruction), which
posits in the simplest form that as long as the United States has enough
nuclear weapons to be able to destroy most of the Soviet population, it does
not matter that the Soviet Union has nuclear superiority. The people
involved realized that life, especially among the superpowers, was more
complicated than that, and yet the emphasis on rigorous, academically
respectable logical analysis prevented academics from investigating what
nations would actually do in times of crises.

Then came Graham Allison's book, *The Essence of Decision.*[2] He set
out to investigate a single incident, the Cuban missile crisis of 1962, against
the background of several disciplines, notably economics and organization
theory. He sought to answer a very simple set of questions, such as why the
Russians placed offensive weapons in Cuba, why we reacted with a block-

ade (rather than, say, a surgical air strike), and why the Soviets backed down. Allison analyzed these questions (admittedly with less than complete information, indeed with only information publicly available). He first used the "rational actor" model that had until then dominated strategic studies (and which is in some ways analogous to the role of maximization in micro-economic analysis). From this model and using the information available, he derived an explanation, indeed several competing explanations, of what actually happened.

Allison then looked more closely at the organizations involved on the U.S. side. (He knew little or nothing about the organizations involved on the Soviet side.) From that inquiry, prompted by organization theory, he derived another set of insights, some reassuring, some hilarious, some frightening. He found, for example, that the Navy blockade did not operate at all the way President Kennedy and his closest advisors planned or even as they thought it was operating at the height of the blockade and, moreover, that the Navy never intended to carry out the blockade in any way other than the way the Navy manuals called for. (An analogy immediately springs to mind of the way government lawyers enforce the antitrust laws, regardless of the wishes of elected Executive Branch officials and the legis-lators who enacted the underlying statute.)

Finally, Allison investigated the political interactions among the top officials actually involved in the Cuba decisions and uncovered still more immensely revealing information and derived some important principles (hypotheses?) about how strategic decisions are actually taken by flesh-and-blood government officials. The overall effect of Allison's book is to emphasize how little we actually know about how decisions are taken by governments and how important the institutional arrangments and even (to commit a law-and-economics heresy) how important the individuals involved are to outcomes.

The effect of Allison's book and of the reactions and controversy it generated on thinking in strategic studies, on the methods of analysis in government and in the think tanks and even on the level of understanding of young government officials recently emerged from the universities is, in my limited experience, quite remarkable.

A comprehensive study of the political economy of antitrust would consequently not be limited to efforts along the quantitative, hypothesis-testing lines suggested by Baxter (even assuming that he fails in convincing us that nothing further can be done along those lines). It would also include a detailed inquiry into the functioning of the different governmental institu-tions involved (including the handling of antitrust cases by the courts and the role of those officers of the court, the treble-damage and defense bars). It would include fairly conventional analysis of the impact of procedural and jurisdictional rules on substantive outcomes.

Such a comprehensive study would seek, moreover, to gain insight into questions of personality, ideology, and elite opinion formation. Do the people who hold positions make any difference (for example, a Kennedy versus an Eastland as chairman of the Senate Judiciary Committee)? Does the existence of a policy planning office in the FTC make any difference and can one tell a Liebeler from a Reich in terms of the cases the Commission brings? Indeed, can one see any influence of Supreme Court opinions, say in *GTE-Sylvania* and now *ASCAP* in the positions taken by the FTC and Antitrust Division staffs? Does scholarly writing have any impact on the decisions of legislators, enforcement officials, and judges? Does the training of judges in economics have any impact on their decisions?—on the language of their opinions? What can one predict about the influence of even the best written and edited *Supreme Court Economic Review?* These are questions which lawyers and economists may not be the best qualified to study. But I would not expect any of us to make a concession publicly.

My prediction is that, in discussing Baxter's paper, this group will come up with several additional hypotheses and reject large numbers of additional suggestions about how he could test his existing hypotheses. I hope that he will ignore our suggestions on that score and turn his efforts to questions about the political economy of antitrust that are more interesting (to me). What I am talking about is the allocation of scarce intellectual resources, and after all, none of us trusts the price system when we deal with ideas that we care about.

Notes

1. Suzanne Weaver, *The Decision to Prosecute* (Cambridge, Mass.: MIT Press, 1977).
2. Graham Allison, *The Essence of Decision* (Boston: Little, Brown and Co., 1971).

5 Commentary:

Oliver E. Williamson

On the Political Economy of Antitrust: Grounds for Cautious Optimism

William Baxter's ambitious effort to assess the forces driving antitrust enforcement is not, as he acknowledges, entirely successful. A leading reason for this is that the data are both crude and incomplete. But there are at least two other factors that contribute to the difficulties. The first of these is that Baxter processes the data relating to his four "political constituencies" in a single-causal way. If, however, antitrust is commonly responsive to multiple rather than single interests, single-causal analysis will predictably yield weak results.

Secondly, and I think more important, Baxter is preoccupied with the realpolitik of antitrust to the exclusion of the possibility that it is *ideas,* as much or more than it is the vested interests, that drive the system. Much of the recent work in the area of regulation has been of the realpolitik kind. Baxter's paper on the political constituency for antitrust is in this same tradition.

But, whereas the vested interests are often easy to identify in the case of regulation, the interests are weaker and more diffuse in the area of antitrust. The development, refinement, and application of ideas are thus apt to be more important. This possibility will be referred to as the paradigm-shift hypothesis.

What has been termed the Keynesian Revolution—which peaked intellectually in the 1950s and enjoyed its greatest influence over public policy in the early 1960s—is an illustration of a major paradigm shift within economics.[1] Shifts of this magnitude, in both the physical and the social sciences, are rare.[2] Indeed, the paradigm shifts to which I have reference here are of a much more localized kind. Specifically, I am concerned with developments in the field of industrial organization over the past forty years. Two paradigm shifts have occured during this interval. The first of these involved a shift away from neoclassical analysis in favor of market-power analysis. The second, and the one that I am mainly concerned with, is the more recent shift in favor of efficiency analysis.[3]

By emphasizing ideas, I do not mean to suggest that vested interests are

77

unimportant. Except, however, as Baxter or others show that the relative power of the interests has changed over time, the distribution of power can be presumed to be constant. The action, therefore, is in the arena for ideas. My examination of antitrust enforcement over the recent past supports, in a general way, the paradigm-shift hypothesis.

Topical comments on Baxter's paper are offered in the first section of this chapter. Some of the institutional factors contributing to enforcement inertia (as contrasted with direction) are examined in the second section. Indications of a paradigm shift in the enforcement of antitrust during the past decade are sketched in the last section.

Some Remarks on Baxter

Hypothesis Testing

Baxter poses four hypotheses for explaining antitrust activity: the private-bar hypothesis, the bureaucratic-aggrandizement hypothesis, the small-firm-resistance hypothesis, and the public-interest hypothesis. The last two are given special emphasis while the first is given short shrift. Baxter regards the suggestion that the private bar encourages misuse of antitrust as "inconsistent with the very substantial evidence that can be gathered from casual empiricism."

Since evidence in this area is difficult to come by, what qualifies as substantial is hard to judge. That there is at least some contrary evidence is plainly suggested by Richard Posner's observation that

> The most distinguished head of the Antitrust Division since Thurman Arnold, Donald Turner, who was responsible for the Merger Guidelines, the increased attention paid by the division to competition in the regulated industries, the upgrading of economists within the division, and the first attempt to exercise a critical review over the trial lawyers' initiatives, was rewarded for his achievements with widespread hostility not only within the division but among congressional supporters of antitrust, other "liberals," *and members of the antitrust defendants' as well as plaintiffs' bar.*[4]

Posner's observations are interesting not only in that they include the private bar as a factor operating against the "public interest" (as Turner and Posner and certainly many others would interpret it), but that the private bar was joined by parts of the career staff and certain politicians whose favored posture for antitrust was one of "vigor." This raises the question of whether the private-bar hypothesis should be dismissed so readily. It also suggests that the multiple causation to which I referred at the outset should be given greater attention than Baxter accords it.

Litigation Model

Baxter's model for assessing private litigation can, I think, be restated to advantage, and a minor improvement effected in the process. Let S_d denote the maximum that a defendant would be willing to pay for a settlement and S_p denote the minimum that a defendant will accept. Using Baxter's notation, these can be expressed respectively as $S_d = P_d D_d + E_d$ and $S_p = P_p D_p - E_p$. The feasibility of a settlement then turns on whether $S_d \lessgtr S_p$. Rational parties will settle if $S_d > S_p$, in which event the settlement range lies between S_p and S_d. If, however, $S_d < S_p$, a settlement cannot be reached and the case will be litigated. Graphically, the situation is shown in the following figure.

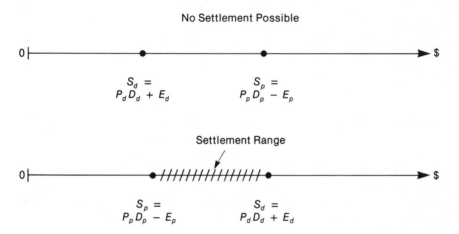

By contrast, Baxter contends that the settlement range is between zero and $S_d - S_p$. Unless I have misinterpreted Baxter or otherwise erred, this is not correct. However, none of this affects Baxter's analysis of the factors favoring settlement. Thus any change in the variables which drives S_p down (namely, an increase in E_p or a decrease in P_p or D_p) or S_d up (namely, an increase of P_d, D_p, or E_d) will improve the prospect of settlement.

As Baxter observes, when both parties have roughly the same perception of the litigated outcome (say, $\bar{L}$), a settlement will always be reached— since then $S_d = \bar{L} + E_d$ always exceeds $S_p = \bar{L} - E_p$. Common perceptions thus promote settlement. For cases that go to completion, judgment for plaintiff or defendant should be split about equally if Baxter's model applies. The data on private actions support the view that perceptions are shared but contradict the equal split prediction. Rather, among those that go to judgment, the defendant is five times more likely to win than the plaintiff. What explains this condition?

Strategic Litigation

Baxter's amended model allows for the possibility that plaintiffs are using litigation as a strategic deterrent to competition. Robert Bork recognizes and expresses the issue as follows:

> Misuse of courts and government agencies is a particularly effective means of delaying or stifling competition . . . The cost of the litigation must be measured against the delay in the appearance of a rival in a lucrative market. The object is . . . to tie him up in proceedings.[5]

Thus even if the plaintiff fully expects to lose ($P_p D_p = 0$), the plaintiff could file a case because deferring competition yields benefits of magnitude (say V) such that $V - E_p$ exceeds E_d—in which case litigation to completion will occur and judgment for the defendant will be reached in a disproportionate number of litigated cases. (As Baxter points out, however, other factors—such as multiple exposure effects on defendants—also contribute to this result).

Security Prices

As Baxter observes, security price movements can sometimes be used to infer antitrust consequences. This is especially true in the merger area.[6] Interestingly, the price movements of *rival* firms will often discriminate between market power and efficiency hypotheses better than will an examination of the security prices of the merging firms.

Again, however, the data problems are apt to be severe. Security prices reflect all of the relevant factors bearing on the fortunes of a firm. Whether it will be possible to pick up movements in security prices that can be confidently attributed to mergers (proposed, permitted, disallowed) seems to me problematical. Greater attention to this area may nonetheless be warranted.

Political Voting Patterns

Baxter's efforts to study political voting patterns to assess which constituencies are being served encounter major data problems. But there are also problems of interpreting what the public-interest hypothesis implies. Although Baxter begins the paper with a statement that the public interest is served when antitrust is used to promote more efficient resource allocation, he appears to drop this position when it comes to studying voting patterns.

Instead, he contends that "the income effects of antitrust enforcement must surely be egalitarian" if the public-interest hypothesis holds.

Doubtlessly there are many who would agree with the latter interpretation. I submit, however, that Baxter's original position ought to be maintained. Not that an equitable distribution of income is an unworthy social goal. The issue, rather, is one of efficacy. Worthy goals and goal achievement ought to be distinguished—especially as goal achievement is commonly promoted by matching public-policy instruments to goals in a discriminating way. To insist that efficiency is the only social goal that antitrust should be concerned with may be unacceptable to many students of antitrust. But that antitrust is poorly suited to promote a more desirable distribution of income is a proposition that Bork has argued often and with which I expect Baxter agrees.

Miscellaneous

I offer only a few further observations, mainly by way of emphasizing points made by Baxter.

Economies of Scale. The economies of scale upon which Baxter's spatial model relies presumably take the form of setup costs. Greater attention to these costs and their consequences is needed, especially as these have a bearing on the condition of entry.

Span of Control. Baxter's reference to span of control raises the more general issue of organizational innovation. Whereas technical innovation receives a great deal of attention, the study of organizational innovation has been relatively neglected. This is unfortunate, since there are reasons to believe that organizational innovations are among the most significant contributions of capitalism.[7]

Negative Results. A great deal can often be learned from negative results, but biases in the publication machinery often preclude this. One of the values of Baxter's study is that the data problems are fully disclosed. Follow-on studies will surely benefit.

Some Sources of Inertia

Two sources of inertia are emphasized here: indoctrination lags and lags in overturning precedent.

Indoctrination Lags

Except as new work on antitrust economics originates within the enforcement agencies, as some does, a highly responsive antitrust enforcement process can do no more than avail itself of the best recent work on antitrust economics. Realistically, this will entail a lag of several years before articles that appear in the law and economics journals show up in the enforcement process. For one thing, cases that are already in progress are difficult to reshape—although more of this should probably be done. For another, more rapid acceptance of new ideas would reflect undue haste; many new proposals require criticism and refinement before applications are warranted.

Typically, however, lags are longer than just a few years. This is because the enforcement of antitrust is mainly controlled by lawyers, and there are long indoctrination lags. The lags are of two kinds. First, there is generally the lag between the time a new economic concept is introduced and the time that it is digested and makes its appearance in books and articles expressly directed at a law school audience. Secondly, even after new economic argument is introduced into law school teaching, there is a considerable lag before recent graduates are in a position to have a strong impact on shaping legal argument—both within the enforcement agencies and the private bar. As a consequence, yesterday's scholarship—which is to say developments which had their origins as much as a decade earlier—tends to be the reference literature.

By way of illustrating the argument, consider the lags that attended entry-barrier analysis and economies as an antitrust defense. Joe Bain's original work on entry barriers appeared in the *Economic Journal* in the early 1950s.[8] His book *Barriers to New Competition* appeared in 1956. Kaysen and Turner's influential *Antitrust Policy,* in which entry barriers and other market-structure measures were prominently featured, followed in 1959. The decade of the sixties witnessed substantial reliance on the entry-barrier concept within the enforcement agencies and in the courts. It was central to the Supreme Court's prohibition of Proctor & Gamble's acquisition of Clorox[9] and "was crucial to the reasoning of the oligopolyphobes of the Neal Task Force."[10] Indeed, since so many economists were uncritical in their use of the concept of entry barriers, and since the entry-barrier concept was such a convenience to zealous enforcement agencies, abuses were rampant. Virtually every impediment to entry was branded as antisocial, and many were made a cause for antitrust relief. As discussed in section 2 below, these abuses have come under control only after another decade of repeated criticism.

As a second illustration of lagged responses, consider my 1968 paper on "Economies as an Antitrust Defense."[11] With a few exceptions, Joe Bain being one,[12] this paper was mainly ignored or met with hostility when it first appeared. It was a full decade later before it made its way into the legal literature—when Robert Bork made extensive use of it in his book *The Antitrust Paradox,* W.J. Liebeler relied on it in his paper "Market Power and Competitive Superiority in Concentrated Industries" in the *UCLA Law Review,* and Terry Calvani and John Siegfried included a variant of this paper in their readings book *Economic Analysis and Antitrust Law.*[13]

To be sure, some of the lags may be shrinking as larger numbers of articles which, at an earlier time, would have first appeared in economics journals are now being published in law reviews. But the generational effects to which I referred earlier will remain. And even if these should shorten, the adequacy of new proposals needs to be tested by academic critique before adoption by practitioners is warranted.

The upshot is that there are some reducible and other irreducible indoctrination lags. Happily, the former kind appear to be shrinking.

Overturning Precedent

Precedents of two kinds are usefully distinguished: legal precedents and administrative precedents. Both are resistant to undoing, though for different reasons.

Upsetting Legal Precedent. Most institutions are reluctant to admit error. This is especially true of conservative institutions, and the courts are surely that. But there are other less widely remarked impediments to overturning legal precedent. These are the problems of mechanics and the defective incentives that operate.

George Hay speaks to the former as follows:[14]

Suppose you are a Supreme Court Justice who has just decided, let's say, a tie-in case, and some months later you pick up the latest issue of *The Journal of Law and Economics* and you read Ward Bowman's analysis that persuades you that your decision was fundamentally in error. (Note in this connection that many of the interesting antitrust economics articles are written in the *wake* of a Supreme Court case.) What is the mechanism by which you would ever get the chance to reverse the erroneous conclusion?

Put differently, examine the process that is set in motion by the original decision. The private lawyer advises his client not to engage in the illegal practice. Should a firm be so uninformed or foolhardy to engage in the process and get caught, the lawyer will advise the client that he might as well settle or plead *nolo contendere.* If the case does go to trial the defense is unlikely to take on directly the economic argument but will try to differentiate his situation or deny having engaged in the process, etc. The point is that the initial decision sets in motion a process by which the courts (or by the same token the economists in the prosecuting agency) are not normally given the opportunity to "correct" the initial error.

Defective incentives exist because each firm consults its own profitability calculus in devising legal strategy rather than consider the collection of firms that are adversely affected by a bad legal precedent. This explains the preoccupation with "market share" games for so many years. Thus rather than display the benefits associated with a merger, which undertaking would require the courts to take a larger view of what was at stake and hence was a risky strategy, successive firms (and their legal counsel) played the merger game on the enforcement agencies' turf. The agency would allege an anticompetitive effect because a merger would exceed some threshold market share (in some product market in some section of the country). The firm would respond that the relevant market was different and that the threshold test statistic was not met. Endless and fruitless disputes ensued, while a serious consideration of the economic purposes of the statute went unremarked.

Since collective action is difficult to mobilize and since each litigant can appropriate only a small fraction of the benefits from correcting a bad precedent, the system is beset with defective incentives. Myopic subgoal pursuit thus operates to preserve rather than reverse bad precedent.

Upsetting Administrative Precedent. Relaxing administrative precedents is also difficult to accomplish. Again the problem is one of defective incentives. Consider the Vertical Merger Guidelines.

Although there is virtually unanimous academic opinion that Vertical Merger Guidelines are too severe, the prospect that these will be relaxed appears to be slight. The adjustment difficulty is attributable to the advocacy posture expected of heads of the Antitrust Division. Any inclination to "soften" the Guidelines would be greeted with alarm by militant antitrusters—within government and without. A failure to execute the advocacy role with vigor would be branded a sell-out.

Thus although the Merger Guidelines perform a useful announcement function for firms and operate as a check against the proclivities of a few zealous staff members who would extend the reach of antitrust beyond reason, the Guidelines (and other administrative pronouncements) have a ratchet effect and thus need to be drawn carefully. If tightening is consonant with role definitions but relaxing is not, original standards ought presumably to err on the side of moderation.

Some Indications of Progress

Although there is an ebb and flow to antitrust, and recent changes may be reversed, it is my judgment that antitrust has made remarkable progress during the past decade—and I would say that a decade is about the appropriate interval at which to take such observations. Some of the areas in which progress has occurred include greater respect for economies in assessing social effects, better understanding of vertical integration and vertical restrictions, a deeper understanding of predatory pricing, greater skepticism with unadorned market share analysis, and a delimitation on entry barrier arguments.

Treatment of Economies

The 1960s opened with the Federal Trade Commission taking the position that the "necessary proof of violation of the statute consists of types of evidence showing that the acquiring firm possesses significant power in some markets *or* that its over-all organization gives it a decisive advantage in efficiency over its smaller rivals.[15] In other words, efficiency and the prospect of extending efficiency were regarded unfavorably by the FTC in assessing whether a merger should be permitted. This perverse use of efficiency reasoning has mainly disappeared since, but vigilance is warranted. The Justice Department made similar arguments in resisting the acquisition of the Mead Corporation by Occidental petroleum in 1978. The government's lead attorney advised the court that the acquisition was objectionable because it would permit Mead to construct a large greenfield plant, which was the "most efficient and cost effective" investment, and that this would disadvantage Mead's rivals.[16]

I am prepared to believe, however, that this contorted view of antitrust economics is an aberration—a manifestation of "creative lawyering" (see section on Market Share Analysis)—rather than a return to Foremost Dairy standards. For the most part, the past decade is one in which greater respect has been accorded to economies, both in the courts[17] and in the legislature.[18]

Parametric analysis of economies versus market-power effects has doubtlessly contributed to this result. Such analysis is useful in two respects. First, it shows the importance of being sensitive to economies if economic rather than emotive consequences are to be accorded serious weight. Secondly, and every bit as important, parametric analysis often permits difficult issues of quantitative net benefit assessment to be bypassed. Thus what difference does it make that demand elasticities are imperfectly known if, throughout the full range of relevant elasticities, the same net-benefit assessment obtains.

Put differently, thinking in net-benefit terms does not require that issues be addressed in fully quantitative terms. Conceptual benefits obtain by simply getting the issues straight, which would have avoided the mistakes made by the FTC in *Foremost Dairies* and by the Antitrust Division in resisting the Occidental-Mead takeover attempt. If tradeoffs are involved, and if a net negative (or a net positive) assessment obtains over the relevant range of parameter values, a "refined" net-benefit assessment is unnecessary. That the matter of economies as an antitrust defense does not elicit the same hostility now that it did in the 1960s is presumably because an appreciation for these conceptual gains, including the power of parametric analysis, is now more widespread.

Vertical Market Relations

The antitrust atmosphere that prevailed in the area of vertical market restrictions in the 1960s was one of hostility. Donald Turner expressed it as follows, "I approach territorial and customer restrictions not hospitably in the common law tradition, but inhospitably in the tradition of antitrust law."[19] Such reasoning was responsible for the mistaken arguments in *Schwinn.*[20]

In an unususal reversal of precedent, the Supreme Court has recently overruled *Schwinn* in the *GTE-Sylvania* case.[21] Among the reasons for this surely has been the growing awareness that "nonstandard" modes of organization usually arise in response to economizing opportunities. Accordingly, except as rather special structural preconditions are satisfied, vertical restraints should not be regarded with animosity.

This position has taken a long time to be recognized. Among the contributing factors was the stream of criticism provided by the Chicago School (Director, Bork, Posner, and others, like Baxter) increasing appreciation for transaction-cost reasoning (Williamson, Phillips), and Turner's dramatic switch of position.[22] That reversals of bad precedent occur in the face of such criticism is surely a healthy indication of progress in antitrust.

Predatory Pricing

The leading predatory pricing case in the 1960s was *Utah Pie.*[23] Although the protectionist reasoning that the Court employed in this case has not been expressly reversed, the unsatisfactory quality of the opinion has been widely remarked[24] and considerable effort has been made to provide a more substantial economic basis for evaluating predatory pricing.

The standards that will eventually emerge are still unclear. As Paul Joskow has observed, the lower courts adopted the Areeda-Turner average-variable-cost rule for evaluating predatory pricing with undue haste:[25]

> First, this rule has not been accorded generally favorable reviews by economists; the rave reviews come from the courts. It does not represent a tri-

umph of economic efficiency over political considerations. Rather, I believe that this rule has attracted so much judicial attention because it provides a way of disposing of cases that have arisen in an area where there are vague and conflicting rules proposed by political antitrusters, that often had to be applied to cases that seemed only to seek the preservation of particular competitors. I attribute the adoption of this particular rule to the desire of the judiciary to extract itself from the chaos of existing case law, not to their "getting religion." I attribute the elegant footnotes to their law clerks. I believe that we are seeing adopted what some of us view as an inappropriate rule from the perspective of economic efficiency because our friends the "political antitrusters" were given too much rope. The courts were presented with vague notions about the value of small business, then were told that they shouldn't confuse individual competitors with competition, saw discussions of bigness *per se* confused with mergers of manufacturing of wooden spoons, heard the phrase competitive process a few times, and were left with nothing useful for coming to a decision. It was almost inevitable that a simple *per se* rule would be eagerly adopted, whether it evolved from appropriate considerations of economic efficiency or not. If average variable cost is a bad rule I suggest that we have it because of the void that was left in this area by the political antitrusters, not because of triumph of economic efficiency considerations in the interpretation of antitrust statutes.

To be sure, the courts were in a difficult bind. Faced with the need to decide cases, the courts could not wait until the Areeda-Turner rule had been tested by academic commentary. Fortunately, however, such commentary has been quick to appear.[26] Much of this has emphasized intertemporal efficiency. The likelihood that better tests for remunerative pricing will be adopted appears to be improving.[27]

Market Share Analysis

When confronted with a difficult case that appears to be beyond the reach of the antitrust statutes, there is a strong temptation to resort to what John Shenefield has referred to as "creative lawyering"[28]—which is a euphemism for bringing a contrived case. Such a temptation is especially great in the merger area, where the language of the statute is very broad. If an adverse effect can be shown "in any line of commerce, in any section of the country," all that a creative lawyer needs to do is define his lines of commerce and geographic markets with sufficient imagination.

Knee-jerk reliance on market-share analysis, however, has also come under increasing criticism. Partly this is a reaction to the arbitrary standards of the sixties and partly it reflects an appreciation that valued economizing purposes are frequently served by reconfiguring economic activity. The degree of disenchantment with a market-shares based approach to antitrust is illustrated by Richard Schmalensee's recent paper dealing with the *Rea-Lemon* case and Darius Gaskin's comments thereon.[29] The economizing purposes served by reconfiguring economic activity have already been remarked in connection with the discussion of vertical market relations. More generally, there is a growing awareness that transaction costs are central to an understanding of the organization of economic activity and that earlier antitrust traditions in which these considerations are ignored or suppressed miss much of what makes a high performance enterprise economy function.

Barriers to Entry

Barriers to entry analysis as a guide to antitrust policy peaked in the 1960s. The term carries an anticompetitive connotation and the more militant members of the barriers to entry tradition plainly believed that any action that had the effect of impeding entry by new rivals or disadvantaging extant firms should be regarded as anticompetitive and should be proscribed. Mergers that yield efficiencies were among the objectionable practices. Advertising economies were held to be particularly offensive. This view was pressed by the government and adopted by the Supreme Court in the 1967 decision regarding the illegality of Proctor & Gamble's acquisition of Clorox.[30]

Confusion on this matter continues to this day. Thus Leonard Weiss, in contrasting Bain with Stigler on barriers to entry, insists that economies of scale be regarded as a barrier; "To characterize such a situation as displaying 'no barrier' is to give the term barrier to entry a meaning that is not very useful in evaluating market power."[31] Why we should be preoccupied with market power to the exclusion of possible economies is not explained, but that is plainly the thrust of entry-barrier analysis and its enthusiasts.

Fortunately, however, matters are changing. Bork, among others, has been instrumental in effecting the shift in emphasis, "The question for antitrust is whether there exist artificial entry barriers. These must be barriers that are not forms of superior efficiency and which yet prevent the forces of the market . . . from operating to erode market positions not based on efficiency."[32] Thus merit outcomes, not structure per se, is what matters. The distinction between remediable and irremediable impediments to entry is important in this regard. Little useful public purpose is served, and a considerable risk of public-policy mischief results when conditions of an irremediable kind—that is, those for which no superior outcome can be realized—are brought under fire.

Remediable impediments, by contrast, are ones which, if removed, would lead to superior social outcomes judged in welfare (not market structure) terms. That this distinction is making headway is disclosed by the recent shift in position by Comanor and Wilson on advertising. Whereas previously they had emphasized the adverse-entry effects of advertising,[33] now they adopt a more symmetrical position and counsel that the effects of advertising should be evaluated in welfare rather than market structure terms, "to the extent that consumer information is increased in the same process that monopoly power is attained, we may be unwilling to adopt specific policy measures directed against the latter for fear of adversely affecting the former."[34] Furthermore, whereas previously the indictment against advertising tended to be quite broad, it is now recognized that the concerns are "concentrated in a small number of industries" where advertising-sales ratios are unusually high.[35] Even here, a presumption of net negative consequences is unwarranted.

What this amounts to is that, here as elsewhere, tradeoffs have to be recognized and that informed public policy will not mindlessly pursue "desirable" market-structure outcomes at the expense of efficiency in its various forms. The view that economies must be recognized as a valid antitrust defense has thus gained ascendancy, despite great initial resistance and a few unreconstructed skeptics. This is a considerable shift from where antitrust enforcement stood in the 1960s. It is the principal basis for my claim that antitrust has witnessed great progress during the past decade.

Concluding Remarks

My review of antitrust developments of the past decade is a relatively encouraging one. Affirmative regard for economies is now widespread and the importance of an economies defense is broadly recognized. This was not the case a decade ago. Vertical market restrictions and other unfamiliar business practices were regarded with suspicion during the 1960s. By contrast, the possibility that nonstandard practices are driven by transaction-cost economies is widely conceded today. Abuses of market-share analysis and barriers to entry arguments are much less common today. When abuses appear, moreover, they are quickly challenged. Thus whereas much antitrust argument was uninformed by rudimentary price theory and economizing notions in the 1960s, the role of microeconomics is securely established and the importance of economizing on transaction costs is widely recognized today.

The credit for this transformation is diverse. The Chicago School's tough-minded insistence that individual organization issues be viewed "through the lens of price theory" is certainly a major contributing factor.[36] Advances in transaction cost reasoning and applications thereof to a variety of antitrust concerns have also been a factor.[37] The growing interest in industrial organization issues among the current generation of micro-theorists has also contributed and, I conjecture, will play an even larger role as efforts are made to sort out what is at stake in the area of strategic behavior—that is, efforts by established firms to take up advance positions and/or respond contingently to rivalry in ways that discipline actual, and discourage potential, competition. Whether such behavior exists, what form it takes, how widespread each type is, and what antitrust ramifications attach thereto, are all open to dispute.

The reshaping of the structure-conduct-performance approach to make it more forward-looking and sensitive to tradeoffs has also contributed to the progress.[38] And the increase in the size and quality of the economics staffs in the Antitrust Division and at the Federal Trade Commission have helped assure that bad economic argument gets recognized quickly and that more sophisticated analysis is brought to bear.

The notion that "ideas, not vested interests" drive outcomes[39] is under-standably attractive to academics. Plainly, however, there are public-policy arenas where this is mainly wishful thinking. In particular, realpolitik is apt to crowd ideas where the vested interests are easily organized and the individual stakes are large. Neither, but especially the former, is often the case with antitrust. Accordingly, ideas matter more for antitrust than for many other public-policy issues.

The upshot is that, although good analysis may not have won, it is surely winning. As recent and future refinements are tested and operation-alized, I am confident that these will have a useful impact on antitrust as well. To be sure, there will be lags. And the hazards of creative lawyering will be with us always. Occasional setbacks notwithstanding, I do not expect the accomplishments of the past decade to be reversed. Vigilance is never-theless warranted. Discovering and exposing efficiency consequences will remain among the leading tasks of antitrust scholars.

Notes

1. Interestingly, it was Keynes who observed that "the power of vested interests is vastly exaggerated compared with the gradual encroach-ment of ideas." J.M. Keynes, *The General Theory of Employment, Interest and Money,* (New York: Harcourt, Brace, 1936), p. 383.

2. See Thomas S. Kuhn, *The Structure of Scientific Revolutions* (Chicago: University of Chicago Press, 1962).

3. For a somewhat similar argument—conducted, however, in the narrower context of "Harvard versus Chicago"—see R.A. Posner, "The Chicago School of Antitrust Analysis," *University of Pennsylvania Law*

Review, 127(April 1979):925–948. For a dissent to Posner's treatment, see R.R. Nelson's comment, which immediately follows the Posner paper.

4. R.A. Posner, *Antitrust Law: An Economic Perspective* (Chicago: University of Chicago Press, 1976) p. 230. (emphasis added).

5. Robert Bork, *The Antitrust Paradox* (New York: Basic Books, 1978) p. 159.

6. For a perceptive discussion of the patterns of security prices that attend mergers, see Henry Manne, "Mergers and the Market for Coporate Control," *Journal of Political Economy* 73(April 1965):110–120.

7. For a discussion of organizational innovation, see Alfred Chandler, Jr.'s two major studies *Strategy and Structure* (New York: Doubleday Inc., 1966) and *The Visible Hand: The Managerial Revolution in American Business* (Cambridge, Mass.: Harvard University Press, 1977). Also see A.H. Cole, "The Entrepreneur: Introductory Remarks," *American Economic Review* 58(May 1968):60–63, and O.E. Williamson, *Markets and Hierarchies: Analysis and Antitrust Implications* (New York: Free Press, 1975).

8. The first statement was Joe S. Bain, "Conditions of Entry and the Emergence of Monopoly," in E.H. Chamberlin, ed., *Monopoly and Competition and Their Regulation* (London, 1954).

9. *FTC* v. *Proctor & Gamble Co.,* 382 U.S. 568 (1967).

10. Bork, *The Antitrust Paradox,* p. 310.

11. Oliver E. Williamson, "Economics as an Antitrust Defense: The Welfare Tradeoffs," *American Economic Review* 68(March 1978):18–36.

12. Joe S. Bain, *Industrial Organization,* 2nd ed., (New York: Wiley, 1968), p. 658.

13. Wesley J. Liebeler, "Market Power and Competitive Superiority in Concentrated Industries," *UCLA Law Review* 25(August 1978):1231–1300; Terri Calvani and John Siegfried, *Economic Analysis and Antitrust Law,* Boston: Little, Brown and Co., 1979.

14. George Hay, "Panel Discussion on the Powers and Limits of Economics for Antitrust," in O.E. Williamson, ed., *Antitrust Law and Economics* (Houston, Tx: Dame Publications 1980), p. 320–325. Reprinted with permission.

15. *In re* Foremost Dairies, Inc., 60 FTC 944, 1084 (1962), emphasis added.

16. The phrase was employed by the government's lead attorney, Barbara Reeves, in support of Count Four (Elimination of Actual and Potential Competition in Coated Free Sheet Paper), *U.S.* v. *Occidental Petroleum Corporation* (Civil Action No. C–3–78–288).

17. For a discussion, see O.E. Williamson, "Economies as an Antitrust Defense Revisited," *University of Pennsylvania Law Review* 125(April 1977):728–729.

18. Ibid, pp. 731–733. An economies defense was also incorporated in the recent no-fault monopoly proposal by the National Commission for the Review of Antitrust Laws and Procedures in its Report to the President and the Attorney General (Washington, D.C., 1979), chap. 8.

19. Turner expressed these views while he was Assistant Attorney General in charge of the Antitrust Division. The statement is attributed to him by Stanley Robinson, 1968 New York State Bar Association, *Antitrust Law Symposium*, p. 29.

20. For a summary of the government's main arguments in *Schwinn* and a critique thereof, see O.E. Williamson, "Assessing Vertical Market Restrictions: Antitrust Ramifications of the Transaction Cost Approach," *University of Pennsylvania Law Review* 127(April 1979):975–985.

21. *Continental T.V., Inc.* v. *G.T.E. Sylvania, Inc.,* 433 U.S. 36 (1977).

22. Turner participated in the Amicus brief with attorneys for the Motor Vehicle Manufacturers Association asking that the *Schwinn* decision be upset. Motion for Leave to File Brief and Brief for Motor Vehicles Manufacturers Association as Amicus Curiae, *Continental T.V., Inc.* v. *G.T.E. Sylvania, Inc.*

23. *Utah Pie Co.* v. *Continental Baking Co.* 386 U.S. 685 (1967).

24. See Bork, *The Antitrust Paradox,* pp. 386–389. Also see Posner, *Antitrust Law* pp. 193–194.

25. Paul L. Joskow, "Comment on The Political Content of Antitrust," in O.E. Williamson, ed., *Antitrust Law and Economics*, 1980, p. xxx.

26. Among the relevant papers are F.M. Scherer, "Predatory Pricing and the Sherman Act: A Comment," *Harvard Law Review* 89(March 1976): 869–890; O.E. Williamson, "Predatory Pricing: A Strategic and Welfare Analysis," *Yale Law Journal* 87(December 1977):284–340; Richard Schmalensee, "On the Use of Economic Models in Antitrust," *University of Pennsylvania Law Review* 127(April 1979):994–1050.

27. Recent court decisions have been more cautious about accepting the Areeda-Turner test that were earlier ones. The Ninth Circuit opinion in *California Computer Products, Inc.* v. *International Business Machines Corp.* reflects this. Memorandum Opinion in *O. Hommel Co.* v. *Ferro Corp.* (Civil Action No. 76-1299) by the U.S. District Judge William W. Knox likewise expresses skepticism with the Areeda-Turner test.

28. Hon. J.H. Shenefield, Testimony before the Subcommittee on Antitrust and Monopolies of the Committee on the Judiciary, United States Senate, July 18, 1978, p. 65.

29. Schmalensee, pp. 1004–1016, and Gaskin, pp. 154–158, in O.E. Williamson, ed., *Antitrust Law and Economics* (1980).

30. Bork, *The Antitrust Paradox,* p. 310.

31. L.W. Weiss, "The Structure-Conduct-Performance Paradigm and Antitrust," *University of Pennsylvania Law Review* 127(April 1969):1121.

32. Bork, *The Antitrust Paradox,* p. 341.

33. W.S. Comanor and T.A. Wilson, "Advertising, Market Structure, and Performance," *Review of Economics and Statistics* (November 1967) pp. 423-440.

34. W.S. Comanor and T.A. Wilson, "Advertising and Competition: A Survey," *Journal of Economic Literature* 17(June 1979):472.

35. Ibid., p. 470.

36. For a development of this theme, see Posner, *Antitrust Law.* Bork's recent book (*The Antitrust Paradox*) is an important contribution to this tradition. The main limitation of the Chicago School has been its reluctance to make allowance for transaction costs, especially as this relates to strategic behavior. For a discussion, see my review of Bork's book in the Winter 1979 issue of the *University of Chicago Law Review* 46(1979): 526-531.

37. For a discussion, see O.E. Williamson, "The Economics of Antitrust: Transaction Cost Considerations," *University of Pennsylvania Law Review* 122(June 1974):1439-1496; also see Williamson, *Antitrust Law and Economics.*

38. See R.E. Caves and M.E. Porter, "From Entry Barriers to Mobility Barriers," *Quarterly Journal of Economics* 91(May 1977): 241-262.

39. Keynes, *General Theory,* p. 384.

Discussion

Baxter on the
Discussants' Papers

Baxter: I guess I have least to say about Brozen's paper, and therefore I'll start there. I was aware of some, but not all, of the empirical studies to which Brozen refers. All save one, however, have their data-base comprised of defendant firms. In thinking about this problem, I have convinced myself that there's an enormous advantage in looking at the securities prices of competitor firms, and therefore the effect on the market, rather than looking at the securities prices of defendant firms.

I was also puzzled by the suggestion in Brozen's paper that the decree might actually have improved the position of United Shoe Machinery; and he will undoubtedly explain to us why Shoe wouldn't have shortened those leases itself if shorter leases were likely to be more profitable.

I have a larger number of points to make about Williamson's paper. First of all, in common with Dam's paper, it starts off by suggesting that I was looking for *the* single cause of antitrust. Going back over my own paper, I can see how one might read it that way. Nevertheless, I never thought that I was going to explain everything with *one* independent variable. As a matter of technique, I thought I'd see if I could find any significant independent variables, keeping in mind that several could be stitched together later into a multivariate form.

Williamson's paper, at a different point, suggests that I shifted my hypothesis. I started off, as he says, and now I think unwisely, identifying one of my hypotheses as the so-called "public-interest" hypothesis. Williamson suggests that this hypothesis might have been better identified as a consumer hypothesis. Normatively, I happen to equate consumer benefits over the long run with the public interest. But that's neither here nor there, because I think we are both trying in our papers to speak in descriptive rather than normative terms.

Later on in my paper I propose to test that hypothesis by reference to income groups, and I suggest that the consumer hypothesis carries with it egalitarian operational effects. I think that's almost bound to be true. I do not regard the proposal to use income as a variable as shifting my hypothesis, but rather as finding testable consequences of the original hypothesis.

The principal theme of Williamson's paper, in common with Dam's paper, is that ideas matter. Williamson gives us a long and interesting recital, one with which I am in almost total agreement, as to how antitrust laws have changed as intellectual understanding of antitrust issues have changed. And I have no doubt that changing intellectual perceptions have affected the rules. It is equally clear to me, however, that ideas are not the only things that matter. Ideas don't matter very much at all, for example, in some regulatory contexts. The next paper that explains why it is that motor carrier regulation is utterly perverse will not make the least bit of difference to the Congress. Motor carrier legislation is the way it is because two very powerful lobbies want it that way—the Teamsters Union and the American Trucking Association. We can give legislatures "ideas" until hell freezes over, and it's not going to change anything. That proposition is less obviously true in the context of antitrust, but it seems to me a perfectly legitimate question to ask how much it is true and how much do other things, such as private interest, matter in the antitrust area.

Dam's paper is rather like Williamson's in some respects. Rather than arguing that ideas matter, Dam argues primarily that individuals and their organizational contexts matter. The relevant question is, of course, how much they matter; no one doubts they will cause some residual variance in the study of antitrust. Nor should we lose sight of the important fact that individuals operate within a context of constraints that tend to push them toward certain kinds of outcomes.

Dam's observations push strongly in the direction of case studies rather than hypothesis testing by larger data sets. I don't view case studies as a hostile and totally different method of scholarship. I know some of you were present just about a year ago, in Philadelphia, where I defended the practice of doing case studies against what I called an unfair assault of the regressionists. And I haven't changed my views on this matter. Good case studies are very productive and are often the best source of testable hypotheses. But until hypotheses are tested, one can never know the extent to which the apparent implications of case studies can be generalized to other cases.

Blake's paper is the one that poses the greatest difficulties for me. The problem, as I see it, is that I proposed the small business model as a testable, descriptive embodiment of Blake's (and other's) concept of antitrust. Blake offers no alternative model as a superior embodiment of his antitrust conceptions. And although I take my model seriously in the paper, I gather that Blake does not. His concepts are not usually cast in the form of a small business model, and he apparently rejects that model as an adequate embodiment. He talks instead about Jeffersonian democracy and maximizing consensus, and similar words; but those are highly abstract goals or objectives, not operational concepts. The question thus becomes, what are the operational characteristics of Blake's approach? Because I refer elsewhere to Blake's approach as "Populist posturing," it is no secret that I don't see much by way of operational characteristics in Blake's approach if it cannot be given the operational content of sheltering small enterprises. And the question I would propose to address to Blake is, what are the operatioal features of antitrust policy, as he sees them, if it is not sheltering small businessmen from efficient, often larger, firms? It does seem to me that the sheltering of small business has at least got to be a tangential effect of Blake's concept of antitrust, but I may misunderstand him in one or more respects.

Discussants'
Responses to Baxter

Blake: My appraisal of Baxter's paper is, first, that he shouldn't have taken on the topic. He should have economized his time by devoting his considerable talents to more productive enterprises. And secondly, that having undertaken it, he hasn't produced much for us. I think he's defeated from the start by his assumption that the topic is one which can be made to respond to the hypothesis that efficiency objectives are the central basis for political support of antitrust.

I come down to the position that other ideas and values have political consequences and that antitrust has had multiple and shifting constituencies over ninety years based largely on those other factors. I agree with Dam that such an approach to political constituencies provides the only basis for understanding the course of antitrust legislation and enforcement policy over time, that is, how antitrust has maintained legislative and budgetary support, and where it has been cut back by the multiple instances of special-interest legislation creating exemptions, for example. But I go further than Dam, I guess, by wondering if the question is really worth asking at all. What is the political constituency for the commerce clause, for example? Or what is the constituency for judicial review of legislation? I don't know what results one would expect in asking these kinds of questions. However, I would think that if one were interested in asking about political constituencies for antitrust, it would be more profitable to look at how special interests seeking antitrust exemptions through legislation—organized pressure groups of the kind that Baxter says are more effective in political action—how they have operated and how legislators have responded to their legislative activities.

I think that's all I have to say about Baxter's paper in general terms. I'm not sure that this is the time to respond to his question about assigning operational consequences to my view of antitrust. I think there are ways in which the antitrust laws can be used to inhibit growth of concentration of economic power without imposing an extensive burden on consumers and without being overly protective of smaller firms. But that is a complex subject, and one that I'm not going to take on here.

Dam: The purpose of my paper was to generate some discussion about methodology. Unlike Blake, my primary concern is not with the allocation of the scarce resource of Baxter, but rather with certain developments in the general area of law and economics. Baxter's paper presents an opportunity to talk about some of these general questions. I am not primarily concerned with methodology, but I am concerned with the possibilities of law and economics as a field. I'm particularly concerned with its quantitative emphasis.

Increasingly, studies in law and economics take the form of a model with a smattering of data, most of which are not data on the subject, but rather data which are proxies for the underlying variables. The results of a regression are then presented in a table, with perhaps a couple of paragraphs of implications thrown in at the end. Such is more frequently the standard form of publication on many of the important research questions in law and economics. I believe that this is an unfortunate development. It is not that I think such papers are not worthy, but I am concerned with the influence, particularly on younger scholars, of the kind of work that is done in graduate study in economics. In my commentary I wanted to try to lay bare what is involved in that kind of work, and Baxter's paper provided an opportunity to do so.

I am concerned that this movement, which is certainly very important in economics and increasingly among lawyers dealing with economic subjects, might lead to a point where important work wouldn't be done, because it wouldn't be considered academically worthy. One of the problems with regression methodology is with the very questions we ask. I don't quarrel with what I would consider the first principle of this approach, which is that one has to state a hypothesis. As long as one is at all adroit, one can convert almost any question into a hypothesis. One of the next steps is that hypotheses must be testable in principle. At this point I think we begin to run into problems. Where I really begin to part company with the regressionists is with the proposition that hypotheses must be quantitatively testable. The only way you can really test something, in this view, is if you have some numbers.

I'm also concerned with the methodology forcing us into preposterous kinds of testing. Because in fact we rarely can get data on what we're really interested in, we must use proxies. I find that some of these proxies are rather bizarre—for example, trying to measure the intensity of regulation by the number of pages in the *Federal Register*, and tests of that character. Since those of you who know anything about the administrative process know that what gets in the *Federal Register* is often unrelated to the underlying substantive activity, you will see why trying to measure regulation through the *Federal Register* is bizarre. But this is just one illustration of what you get into, once you're forced toward quantitative measurement and therefore forced to use proxies.

The point that we really want to understand in this conference is the political economy of antitrust. We want to understand how the process functions, and one doesn't get at that issue by trying to break down the variance into constituent explanatory variables. There are a variety of approaches and underlying literatures that one may look at to obtain ideas. For example, there are a great number of questions that one can begin to pose if one takes a historical view of one's subject. Today many scholars are moving away from the notion that we ought to try to understand the development of the antitrust laws over time. Yet it would be useful if we went back and did more work now with regard to some of the historical questions that developed with the Sherman Act. Some of this work has been done before, but it has been done by people who either didn't have any questions they were trying to answer, or by people who not only had the questions but also the answers before they turned to the historical record.

The great problem here is that what we're really interested in is the question of legislative process. We are interested in the enforcement process, in which some work has been done, but not very much. What's interesting today is the relationship between these two things. For example, I have been following fairly closely the whole question of the way in which the FTC, the Antitrust Division, the Senate staffs, and other groups interact with regard to the question of oil companies. For example, what is the push behind the various bills with regard to the dismemberment of oil companies, oil mergers, and conglomerate mergers? Why do those bills not pass? What is the constituency against them? Why is it that thus far they are being blocked? Why is it that the FTC dropped the big oil case in 1973, and why is it that they don't seem to be able to bring the case to trial? Consider also the new form of proceedings embodied in the recent Federal Trade Commission rule-making proceeding which would do with one stroke of the pen much of what the vertical divestiture bill would have done, which is to require all oil companies to divest themselves of pipelines. It's very clear that what is involved here is that certain people in Congress, who are unable to pass the vertical divestiture bill, seek to accomplish the same result by pushing the Federal Trade Commission into promulgating a rule, and hoping that it will hold up all the way through the Supreme Court. These are extremely interesting and important questions, and it's not going to be easy to learn much about them—certainly not by quantitative studies.

I will say with regard to one point that Baxter made that I don't believe that individuals as such matter all that much. I do believe, on the other hand, that particular individuals have become important because they represent particular groups or ideologies. When they reach a position of power, whether it is in Congress or in the enforcement agencies, they are subject to enormous constraints. It's not clear that any one person representing a particular constituency is going to be any more or less effective than another representing the same constituency.

What I do want to argue affirmatively is that we need not only quantitative studies, but also case studies and historical studies. It seems to me there is much work being done in political science now on the use of both quantitative and qualitative measures that are useful to analyze some of the problems in which we are interested. I'm not particularly familiar with this work, but I suspect that people in law and economics tend to dismiss all political science work too easily.

Brozen: I have some of the same sentiments that Dam has expressed, partly for somewhat different reasons, partly for some of the same reasons. One is that the sovereign always has to be all things to all men. And so you have very disparate lines of things appearing. You have a Congress that is interested in protecting the small business, and they push legislation or at least push enforcers of legislation in directions that will protect small business. Yet simultaneously they will do something like passing minimum wage legislation which knocks small business in the head. This is an all things to all men kind of an approach, dispensing favors to some and at the same time dispensing offsetting favors to others. This type of behavior fuzzes up any attempt at quantifying the governmental process.

Another aspect of this that fuzzes analysis is logrolling. If you want to count votes in Congress, how many of those votes are a trade for some other vote? Such problems tend to get in the way of trying to quantify the counting of the constituency, drawing lines on constituencies, who stands for what, and so forth.

Then there is also the tension that exists between Congress, the staff people in Congress, and the antitrust enforcers. You can see some of that going on right now where Congress is voting for a veto over some Federal Trade Commission activities. Why is the Federal Trade Commission doing things that led to this Congressional action? Why is it that we're getting the Federal Trade Commission apparently charging off in one direction while Congress and the administrators are not charging off in that direction? You see this sort of tension in the anecdote in my paper about the small bottlers with exclusive territories that the Federal Trade Commission is attacking. As soon as the small bottlers learned of this attack, they got on the backs of their Congressmen, and you had 106 bills dropped into the Congressional hopper to stop the attack. If the Congress is that interested in stopping the attack, why did the Federal Trade Commission attack in the first place? But then you come back to the fact that none of those bills have passed yet. They were dropped in the hopper five years or six years ago and have been renewed in each Congress since that time.

I wonder how much of antitrust legislation is a ceremonial waving of hands in the air. We have a terrible problem of inflation (or anything else), so let's pass more antitrust legislation. Why antitrust legislation and why not something else that would make a difference to inflation? It seems to me in part that antitrust legislation has as much heat generated around it in congressional hearings and maybe as little passed as is passed because it is a very cheap way of making a gesture. The whole antitrust arena appears to be a kind of charade. As a charade, it is moderately costly and moderately inconsequential as far as any specific results are concerned, excepting perhaps the enrichment of the antitrust bar and the enrichment of those who receive treble damages.

I've attached a table from Ellert's dissertation to my paper which I think demonstrates the point. (See table 3-1.) You will notice that, looking at some of the data in the table, the only place that antitrust apparently has really made any difference is where there are treble damage actions that follow on subsequent to the formal complaints and formal findings. In the table, you see that where a complaint is followed by private suits is where you really get a difference, that is, a statistically significant 16.2 percent loss of stockholder wealth. In any other instance that you want to look at there, whatever line you want to pick, there's very little significance to any of the cumulative residuals. There are small changes in stockholder wealth, but you can attribute that change in stockholder wealth to the cost of defense against the complaint that's brought. Of course, one might be puzzled by the fact that, where you had complaints followed by private suit, the loss of stockholder wealth was not reflected at the time that the complaint was brought. Why didn't it get reflected at the time the complaint was brought? All I can say is that evidently for the period of the survey here, the market was inefficient. What other conclusion can you draw?

Overall, Ellert's results support the notion that by and large antitrust is a charade. The conspiracy cases are not followed by much loss of stockholder wealth, except for the cost of defense in the case, which suggests that the conspiracies were ineffective in the first place and therefore there wasn't much to be lost by discovery of the conspiracy. And if you look at what went on before the case was brought, you'll find that there's no stockholder wealth being gained during the eight and one-half years before the case was brought. If any conspiracy was formed and brought any increase of stockholder wealth, it should have appeared in the period of time surveyed, and it doesn't. There is no statistically significant increase of stockholder wealth due to conspiracies and no statistically significant diminution of stockholder wealth following the dispelling of the conspiracy. The only significant loss of stockholder wealth occurs as a consequence of the defense against the conspiracy charge.

The other thing that's striking is the particular studies on mergers. It appears that the mergers which do the most to improve efficiency in the use of assets are the ones that get dissolved. And the mergers that do the least to improve the efficiency of the administration of assets are the ones that don't get dissolved or don't get attacked. All the more reason for me to believe that antitrust is either a charade or damaging and certainly not helpful to anybody.

Williamson: I find myself in agreement with Professor Dam on the issue of empirical research in the area of antitrust policy. Most of the useful insights that have been produced in this area have resulted from microanalytic case studies. The recent work of Alfred Chandler on business history is also important. Chandler doesn't really address himself to antitrust, but his work does have interesting ramifications for antitrust.

It is important that we get our conceptual foundations straight. One of the problems of jumping too quickly in doing empirical studies is that the conceptual foundations haven't been worked out adequately. Occasionally, it will suffice to simply bring price theory to bear. But frequently we need greater sensitivity to economic processes and historical developments when studying business practices, particularly in the area of vertical integration, vertical market restrictions and issues of price discrimination. There's an enormous amount of research that can be done, and has been going on, once the appropriate microanalytic foundations have been laid. Not only will more appropriate kinds of empirical testing result, but it will also permit us to direct our antitrust resources in a more productive way.

I subtitled my remarks as "cautious optimism" about antitrust developments. The inhospitability orientation toward vertical market restrictions that prevailed in the 1960s has recently been revised as a result of a better understanding of how markets function in terms of transaction cost considerations. Much of the animosity toward product differentiation and advertising during the 1960s has similarly given way to greater sensitivity toward the possible beneficial effects that are associated with such activities. Efficiency as well as market-power effects thus come under scrutiny. I see these developments as definite signs of progress in the antitrust policy area. As a consequence of sharpening up the conceptual foundations, ideas have made headway.

Additional conceptual work remains for the future. But I'm convinced that the changes that I've described here are cases where ideas, rather than vested interests, have been driving the system. The fact that antitrust assessment does not frequently involve vested interests makes it ideologically a much more satisfying area for research.

Dialogue between Baxter and the Discussants

Baxter: I'm not sure I have much of a rebuttal that I want to make. References have been made to my despair. The lesson I learned most clearly from my exercise of the past six months is that one should never undertake to do an empirical project by a deadline. I despair only because I ran out of time.

I really don't think, having worked at it, that we're going to find that there is much information content in litigation win-loss ratios, as Brozen suggests. It appears that there is a bias operating in the settlement process to filter out information that is potentially useful. I despair, if you wish, of pursuing that idea fruitfully.

Having made a careful attempt at legislative hearing witness counting, who shows up and testifies, I'm reasonably well satisfied that there is not much useful information in this approach. Hearings are orchestrated by committee chairmen. A hearing is a deliberately constructed Irish stew: what predominates is what the chairman wants to predominate, but everybody appears to be represented. I don't think there's much information content there.

I feel quite differently, however, about securities prices and voting patterns. I believe that there is a good deal of mileage to be had by looking up data on securities prices and examining the impact of antitrust developments on rival firms. The impact on a rival firm tells us something useful, whereas one cannot be at all sure that the securities price impact on defendant firms tells us anything interesting.

And, similarly, I think there may well be significant information content in voting patterns. I think that the House of Representatives votes are more promising data sets for several reasons. For one thing Senators are always running for president. They see their constituency as national, and hence there is both less variance across Senators and less significance in the characteristics of their voting constituency. It's also a problem in the Senate that you have only 100 observations, as opposed to 435 in the House, and the voting constituencies are inevitably much more homogeneous. In the House, with 435 observations on many roll-call votes over many years, one has a lot of potential explanatory power. I'd be amazed if something can't be drawn out of such data. Furthermore, I really disagree that logrolling is going to obscure this data. As Brozen pointed out, the people whose votes are going to be bought in this market are those who can sell it at the lowest political cost. Such an effect should come through in the data.

I would agree with the implications of Dam and Williamson that statis-

106

tical tests can be overdone. They can be overdone in two quite different ways. One is where you don't have adequate samples: results may not be statistically significant even when they are powerfully suggestive intuitively. The other is where you have an enormous sample size, and you get significant results, nevertheless you may be explaining so little of the total variance, although the results are statistically significant, that they are not of much interest. Accordingly, empirical work, like anything else, involves matters of judgment. There are all sorts of games you can play with statistics. But none of these difficulties convinces me that efforts of this general type are not worthwhile. At the same time, I feel that case studies are among the most likely sources, if not the most likely source, of appealing hypotheses with which one can work.

Dam: Roll calls, particularly if compared with roll calls on other kinds of legislation outside the antitrust realm, can be a useful source of information on what some of the tradeoffs in the logrolling process might have been. Such work represents a very large task. Some has been done in political science. I don't know whether or not you looked at that possibility.

Baxter: I certainly haven't seen any such work on antitrust, or even as Blake suggested, and as I had in mind, on exemption legislation such as the Capper-Volstead and McCarren-Ferguson Acts. And when I say antitrust legislation, of course, I do not have in mind only the roll call, if indeed there was a roll call, by which the eventual piece of legislation was actually passed by the House. During the course of the debate on the bill, there'll typically be a number of amendments proposed from the floor. I think that regression results on some of those proposed amendments, including those that were defeated, often will be more instructive than the final vote on the bill; because by the time of the final vote, everybody knows which way the wind is blowing, and you've got a lot of people voting for the record. Whereas they're usually voting for real on the intermediate proposed amendments, and one tends to get a truer picture of underlying positions.

Dam: Committee voting is also important, because in nearly all legislation the crucial votes are in committees, not on the floor. However, you have smaller numbers, which restrict the possibilities for statistical inference, and therefore qualitative judgments are necessary. You cannot just use a cookbook test. What one has to do is to use statistics in aid of a much more institutionally-oriented study, in which you actually look at the process by which particular exemptions or other statutory provisions were passed. Then, you can begin to see the tradeoffs in the committee itself.

Blake: I think that's a point that is worth emphasizing. It does seem to me that what Williamson said about the theory not being sufficient to support the weight of the data collection and analysis becomes important at this point, and it seems to me that an institutional study would be more productive. One could canvass members of the staffs of the various Senate and House committees and subcommittees who handle antitrust legislation to find out what they have perceived their positions to be with respect to specific proposed legislation, what they thought they could trade for what, which legislators they perceived as allies or opponents, and what in the nature of the constituencies of such legislators they believe to be the reason for their positions. Out of this kind of case study and hypothesis-formation exercise, it seems to me that one could obtain more finely tuned and interesting hypotheses than the ones we have before us.

Brozen: There's one thing that troubles me in looking at roll-call votes, and that is that whether or not the vote really represents the interest of the constituency. There is a learning process at work in some of these things, and constituencies frequently are ignorant of what the effects are going to be. It isn't until after they live with it for a while that they discover it isn't going to turn out to be what they thought. I think you have to couple this with looking at later revisions. Once people learn that the effects of gasoline price controls are that you end up paying a lot more in waiting time in lines than you would pay at the gasoline pump, they revise what they want out of their Congressman or their price controller. We thus not only want to look at votes at a given point in time; we want to see the evolution of votes and the revision in votes as people learn from their experience.

Williamson: I don't have any special thoughts about roll calls, but I do think that Baxter's suggestions on using securities price data are promising and interesting. One of the tricky problems of working with securities prices is there are some difficult anticipation features, and one has to be prepared to make allowance for those. I think that this can be done.

Blake: And there is certainly a problem in the securities prices approach with respect to multiproduct firms, particularly conglomerates, in expecting stock market prices to reveal much about the response to competitors of antitrust proceedings involving only one division or component.

Baxter: Well, in that regard we do have the line of business reports now.

Brozen: The line of business reports is, however, a very truncated set of data. We really need industry data if you're going to do that kind of thing, not the data on two or three large firms in the industry. Secondly, we need the kind of data that you'll never get from the line of business reports, such as data on who got killed, data on investment in the period before firms failed, and how much was written off by the firms who are still in the industry. Such data are never going to show up unless you get a kind of census of business that we've never had. So I can't see that you get anything useful out of line of business reports as currently conceived.

Baxter: All of Brozen's comments are quite right, although I'm not as negative as he is about any prospect for usefulness of this data. In a lot of industries, notwithstanding the fact that data reports are truncated, a substantial fraction of the entire industry is covered by the reports.

Dam: We talked about antitrust largely as though the subject was exclusively how the legislature makes up its minds. We also want to concern ourselves with the enforcement agencies. I want to raise two different kinds of questions. Staying for the moment with the legislature, one set of questions involves what factors go into the legislative decision with regard to what the enforcement agency will be? It's interesting to me, for example, with regard to the present oil merger bill, which is before the Senate Judiciary Committee, that the decision has been made by the staff and by the senators who are pushing it that there should be no Federal Trade Commission jurisdiction and no private enforcement. I assume that they reached that conclusion because they recognize that this is not legislation designed to promote efficiency, and they don't want it to be too costly. It would thus be rather interesting to find out how these questions are perceived in the Congress, and what factors go into the decision on where the enforcement power should be.

One area in which the locus of enforcement issue became of extreme importance was in the consumer protection agency bills, where the very idea of enforcement process became front and center. Now this was not precisely antitrust, but it was a related area.

The second set of questions concerns the behavior of the enforcement agencies. How do they function? How do they select their cases? These are important questions. In fact, they may be more important than what the underlying legislation is.

Suzanne Weaver's book on this subject (*The Decision to Prosecute*)[1] is quite instructive. It addresses the question of how the Antitrust Division selects its cases. Of course, case selection isn't the only relevant consideration. There are also questions of how broad the case will be, whether the enforcement agency is prepared to settle, whether the agency prefers a precedent, the way in which the case is litigated, and so on. Weaver's book is limited because she had to rely exclusively on interviews. She had no access on any systematic basis to the underlying documents. But, nevertheless, the book is filled with insights. It seems to me that this enforcement area is of great importance, perhaps of greater importance than the legislative area.

This is one of the major points that I want to make, namely, the political constituency issue is just a small part of the political economy of anti-trust.

Let me also address one other matter. Williamson has argued, in so many words, that we have more rationality now because of the progress of ideas. Well, during the 1960s we had a situation in which the Supreme Court mindlessly endorsed whatever the enforcement agencies did. But that began to break down as the lawyers' mentality of pushing the law to points where it became absurd began to come to the fore. Now in the merger area, this happened in the *General Dynamics* coal mining case. If you looked at the numbers, it was absolutely clear that there ought to be a violation. Yet, if you looked at the institutional structure of the industry, it was obvious that this merger certainly had no competitive harm. And the Supreme Court simply didn't go along with the Antitrust Division's numbers approach. The only reason it didn't go along, incidentally, was because the counsel had decided that they were not going to cave in and that they were going to fight the case on the facts. They believed, like all good litigators, that facts mat-ter, and their facts were facts about long-term contracts with utilities and similar institutional factors. As a result of *General Dynamics,* therefore, the enforcement authorities now have to come up with something more than just the number of firms and their market share. So they have begun to be more concerned with efficiency. To a certain extent the same thing has hap-pened in section 1 cases, where the mindless application of per se rules had put the antitrust system in the position of striking down arrangements that had obvious efficiency justifications.

So perhaps it isn't really the progress of ideas as such, but rather it is a response to the case-selection process, where enforcement agencies are prone to look for cases where they can advance the area of illegality. That is the way lawyers like to select cases, but it has its own natural offsetting and compensating process in the courts. The agencies bring ridiculous cases, and even the judges can see that they're ridiculous and they find some way to limit the thrust of such activity.

Brozen: How much bad antitrust law, bad in the efficiency sense, is the result of simply lousy defense in earlier cases?

Dam: I think a great deal of it is, though once you say lousy defense, I'm not so sure that some of the criticisms that we academics make of defense lawyers are quite correct. That is to say, it may be a lousy defense from the standpoint of the economy and not necessarily a lousy defense from the standpoint of defendants. That's a question of judgment. Defense lawyers tend to accept the principle of previous cases, and they try to argue that the particular facts in their case are an exception or have to be looked at differ-ently. Such behavior allows the dominant paradigm to continue in place until it is extended so far that it becomes ridiculous, in which cases it collapses.

Williamson: Although I think that there is a lot more economics involved in the decision-making processes in most of the antitrust agencies now, I agree that an advocacy posture tends to prevail, and it takes a long time for the senior career staff to be replaced by younger people with different views of what the nature of the game is. I nevertheless think that changes in the way that they perceive their roles have been real, even though it hasn't been a revolution. These people don't like to do really inane things. Once there's a general recognition of the mistakes that have been made in the past, successive attorneys-general do not want to continue to make them and have their regimes held up to ridicule.

Manne: I've been actively engaged now for three years in administering economics programs for federal judges. In this process we've seen some fairly dramatic illustrations already of how judges can better understand the evidence that was being presented to them. Judges themselves have said that they now understood much more clearly what the expert witnesses were saying and were able to engage them in dialogue. So in this very basic sense, ideas have mattered. Indeed, in a case this past year in the Northern District of California, a district judge included both an average-variable cost and a marginal-cost curve in a footnote to the opinion and discussed those with rather considerable sophistication.

Blake: I'd like to ask Baxter if the discussion today would lead him to reformulate his hypothesis in a way that involves a less ungenerous assumption about why the antitrust bureaucracy acts as a constituency for the antitrust laws? I doubt if the reason is exclusively, or largely, empire-building or moving up the scale of salary grades.

Baxter: I think that when you're looking at these agencies, you have to make a sharp distinction between the professional staffs and the semipolitical appointments who come in at the top of the staffs. If you go down and question one of the chief litigators in the Antitrust Division, he would tell you in all honesty that he had no interest whatsoever in expanding his staff or budget, except for the purposes of doing good. And Blake's suggestion that they believe very deeply in what they're doing is certainly right. Nevertheless, I'm more attached to operational consequences, and therefore to articulating things in the way that one can observe and perhaps even test. Thus, I tend to view the consequence of a commitment to doing good as almost always carrying the implication that there should be more people doing it and that the budget should be bigger.

Dam: May I suggest a different hypothesis about that issue based, not on my knowledge, but on what Suzanne Weaver says in her book (*The Decision to Prosecute*). She says that you can break down the staff of the Antitrust Division into people over 50 and under 40, there being almost nobody there between 40 and 50. The people over 50 went there, not because they liked antitrust, but because they got a job there. They then developed an identification with antitrust. These people believe in antitrust because it's their job.

Among the people under 40, she wasn't able to find anyone who wanted to stay there. They all were planning to go out to private practice. And this fact forms one of the reasons why they're interested in ideas. They believe that ideas might be useful when they get to private practice. Such facts tell us important things about the process of antitrust.

Williamson: It is also useful to look at the historical development of business enterprise. In this respect I think that Chandler's book, *The Visible Hand,*[2] is of some interest. He describes the organization of the railroads in the nineteenth century. The railroads recognized the interdependence they had between them and made successive efforts to try to organize. They tried various sorts of interfirm strategies, but each time these things would break down. It wasn't until they merged that they were able to really consolidate their interests and operate effectively with respect to their market in a concerted way.

Additionally, I think that international comparisons are useful here. Michael Montias, who is in the comparative-systems area, has looked at cartel behavior in pre-World War II Germany and after the allied occupation and the introduction of antitrust statutes and the delegalization of cartels. He reports that nontrivial consequences were associated with this latter process. I would think that instead of simply processing the data in terms of contemporary economic affairs, one can go back and use history and international comparisons to advantage. And such as it is, it seems to me that both these studies suggest that antitrust is more than a charade.

Manne: Let me take issue with Blake's point that business investment in opposing antitrust to some extent moves in the direction of disproving the so-called charade theory. I don't think that's necessarily true. It seems that everyone has to play the game. The idea of calling it a charade is that everyone is acting out some role, and the implication, if I understand what Brozen had in mind here, is that the aggregate quantitative significance of this game has been grossly exaggerated. Also, Williamson argues that things seem to be improving, and this seems to contradict the charade theory. But I would observe that significant improvement may be going on very rapidly within the academic and intellectual communities, while out in the rest of the world, the costs to shareholders and firms of lawyers and such aren't terribly significant.

Brozen: Let me raise a further paradox that puzzles me. Most of these conspiracies show up as having very little positive influence on the value of the firm. Now why do firms engage in these futile efforts? Why do they spend resources in getting together if there's so little positive effect that comes of it? I've tried to resolve this in my own mind in terms of the idea that there's always a hope that maybe one's collusive partners will be suckered into raising their prices, so that one firm can grab the business through secret price-cutting. For example, something like this seems to have occurred in the electrical equipment conspiracy, with General Electric having lost a lot of business to cheating fellow conspirators. They got suckered in, and that's also happened on occasion with the other conspiracies I've looked at. Does that resolve the paradox?

Baxter: Let me address myself to that paradox. I guess I'm not talking here so much as an academician but as a practitioner. In the typical price-fixing case, the active participation stops at or below the hierarchical level of the vice-president in charge of sales or marketing. And even more frequently, it stops at the regional or district manager level. In this setting I don't think it's terribly hard to explain why price conspiracies come into existence. The company's sales force is scattered over some large portion of the nation; it has enormous span of control problems; the sales force is usually operating on a commission basis; there are very strong incentives to restrict price competition. Couple this with the fact that sales people from different companies out on the road tend to stay at the same hotels, eat at the same restaurants, drink together, and so on, and you have a very ripe environment for price conspiracy. So much price-fixing occurs at field-sales-force levels. And it occurs among people who have quite unambiguous incentives to engage in that behavior and who have very little corporate responsibility.

Brozen: I agree, but I'm asking why do they engage in these futile efforts that don't benefit the company?

Dam: They may benefit, but if you're going to measure the effect on securities prices, you're simply not going to pick it up. It's too unimportant. Isn't is also true that price-fixing is more apt to occur in a situation in which the price structure is deteriorating and particularly where the minor executives are being compensated on a profit-center basis related to their own performance? Even where these executives know that there may be some legal risk involved, the incentive to collude is much stronger under such circumstances.

A question: Is the charade theory the same as the theory that says that antitrust is really about symbols? The symbols have very broad electoral appeal, and they're also very important to people who feel that it's important to have antitrust to avoid comprehensive regulation or even nationalization of industry. For example, one of the reasons that the Antitrust Division budget keeps moving up in the President's budget is because a lot of people in the Executive Office of the President are very suspicious of the Federal Trade Commission. They don't want the Federal Trade Commission to take over the antitrust area.

Notes

1. Suzanne Weaver, *The Decision to Prosecute* (Cambridge, Mass.: MIT Press, 1977).
2. Alfred D. Chandler, *The Visible Hand: The Managerial Revolution in American Business* (Cambridge, Mass.: Harvard University Press, 1977).

Economic Aspects
of Antitrust

Schwartz: One distinction has occurred to me that was not made in Baxter's paper and that might conceivably be useful both in terms of empirical work and sorting out the theoretical apparatus. At least I tend to distinguish sharply between a theory of antitrust that asks the question whether the behavior in attempting to secure monopoly power was improper from the question of whether monopoly power had been exercised to the detriment of a class of consumers. I take it that it is the former area of antitrust with which this group has the greatest unhappiness with the theoretical underpinnings. This is the area in which the growth in enforcement seems to be the most dubious. I wonder if one could detect some kind of secular change in the extent to which antitrust enforcement was of this Section 2 kind? I don't think, incidentally, whatever the political answer is, that it's a one-time answer. In other words, you've got a constant political war going here. If you've found that antitrust enforcement both in the private and public sector has become substantially more on behalf of competitors claiming to have been excluded as compared to consumers who were allegedly overcharged, would you know something when you're all through?

Baxter: I guess I wouldn't really agree with your premise that those are the most suspect areas of antitrust. I don't like the Section 2 language. I'd rather speak in terms of the investment phase and exploitive phase of monopoly.

I think there's a perfectly respectable role for predatory-pricing theory, or what I have in the last year or two come to call predatory-limit pricing, deriving largely from Williamson's paper. The sharp dichotomy you suggest isn't one that appeals to me. On the other hand, this kind of investment in predation, like any other kind of investment, must pay off within a relatively short time horizon, or it just cannot conceivably be profitable. And if it's not profitable, then I don't believe very much of it occurs. So that by looking at substantial time horizons, it seems to me that one ought to be able to identify, in terms of rates of return, these investment phenomena, as well as the exploitive phenomena. But predatory investment is not likely to occur unless there is, or at least plausibly expected to be, a subsequent exploitive phase.

Schwartz: As a consumer of economic expertise, it would seem to me that in what we can roughly call the Section 2 theory, or what you call the exploitive phase, the state of the economic art, whatever you can say about it, is much less certain. There is great disagreement among the economists in distinguishing between efficient behavior and exclusionary behavior, to use your words. The ability of competitors to use the laws in a strategic fashion seems intuitively to be very great in this area. You can also point to any number of changes in the substantive law, such as Bigelow, making a proof of damages easier.

So for a variety of reasons on the antitrust landscape, it looks like the initial investment phase has increasingly become the focus of attention. And the question might be fruitfully put, who stands to gain from the shift? It looks to me, offhand, to be the competitors who stand to gain unambiguously from an expansion of antitrust in that direction.

Baxter: I understand what you're saying, but I guess I do not agree that there has been a shift of emphasis in the direction of bringing antitrust to bear on the investment phase. I think it's been there all along. I think, if anything, it has receded somewhat, precisely because of some of the difficulties you identify. Nevertheless, I don't think there's as much disagreement as you suggest among economists, at least at a high level of generality. I may rapidly be proved wrong, by the assembled company, but I think all economists agree that predatory pricing is a real possibility, given certain strategic circumstances. They disagree on whether it happens often, sometimes, or almost never.

But I certainly agree that it's very difficult to frame an administerable rule governing predatory pricing; the probabilities of error once the courts get their hands on the problem are very high. But I don't see any general pattern in antitrust indicating that more attention is being accorded to the investment phase of monopolization than previously was accorded. It has always been a major theme and always less well handled by courts than the exploitive phase.

Brozen: I have difficulty in understanding the predatory pricing argument. First, I see the large firm as being able to raise capital less expensively than a small firm. That in itself tends to make them more efficient necessarily, unless there's some offsetting efficiency in the small firm to offset their inefficiency in raising capital. The latter is obviously true because small firms do survive in competition with larger firms. The major objection to the predatory pricing argument is, however, simply the belief that the large firm will accept a smaller return because it can raise its capital less expensively.

I would like to add a supplementary point to this discussion about the increasing rationality of antitrust. At least in the official enforcement agencies, Robinson-Patman has kind of died down. Unfortunately, the people who like to collect treble damages have become the enforcers of Robinson-

Patman after the enforcement agencies have learned that this is an irrational activity. So we have the continuation of an inefficient piece of the law through private action. Perhaps getting rid of treble damages would help rid us of inefficient legislation.

Schwartz: I can't help choosing this occasion as a consumer of economics to register a complaint. The apparent supposition is that in many important respects the policy issues of antitrust have been materially clarified in the post-Director revolution. However, it seems to me that the underlying fundamental issues in antitrust remain substantially indeterminate. Take the issue of collusion. If I understand correctly, what you want to be able to predict is the degree of collusion which will occur in various sets of circumstances, and all that I have ever seen in this regard is a long laundry list of factors predisposing industries to collusion. As far as I know, no operable theory exists to predict the incidence of collusion. It seems to me that you are back in all the important areas to substantial indeterminancy, that is, you cannot tell in general or in particular what the consequences of a particular economic arrangement are likely to be. I am wondering, that if the state of the economic art is so uncertain, whether we aren't justified in indulging some other preferences that we might have, be it Jeffersonian democracy or whatever.

Gellhorn: You must also examine why the law is changing and where the pressure for change is coming from when the results have been inefficient. A good illustration for this process is the change of rules on vertical restraints in *GTE Sylvania*. While the court left an exception for resale price maintenance, it moved in the direction of the criticisms offered, now recognizing that vertical restraints may enhance efficiency. Here the underlying economic studies have been specific and direct.

Eckert: More generally, some of the propositions that have come forth from the study of the common law suggest that the greater the inefficiency of some decision or some body of decisions, the greater the incentive of parties to challenge these decisions and to bring forth a reversal of them. Now, if certain outcomes of the antitrust laws are more inefficient than others, we should see more resources devoted to and eventually greater likelihood of changing these decisions. Thus an important question is what have been the incentives of the parties most directly affected by antitrust inefficiencies to change that system in a way similar to the way that common law may be changing or may have changed.

Williamson: Although you may not like the laundry list, such a list helps to identify cases where collusion is more likely and that may have a long history of collusive experience. Moreover, it shifts attention away from other industries where the likelihood of this kind of collusion is much more problematic.

As to the exactitude of measurements, I don't see the importance of getting exact measurement if, over a wide range of parameter values, which everybody agrees includes all the relevant values, we reach the same policy result.

With respect to transaction costs, one of the things that needs to be done is to take more care in establishing dimensions of transactions. What are the critical dimensions of transactions? Some progress has been made on this question. I think additional progress will be made, but we are definitely in a position to ask questions now in a more informed way than we were in the mid-1960s.

Baxter: I agree with Williamson. Laundry lists are not very satisfactory, but unless you're ready to give up on antitrust completely, and I'm not, they are the best we can do at present. Cartels represent a real problem. While I am very skeptical about what are traditionally called entry barriers, I am also skeptical about the speed with which entry occurs into capital-intense industries with high profit rates. The transitional losses that occur while we wait around for a new aluminum company to enter a cartelized industry can be very substantial. Once you have conceded that antitrust is going to be brought to bear on explicit collusion, one runs into some nasty procedural and evidentiary problems. There will rarely be eyewitness testimony even when explicit collusion actually occurred, and the circumstantial evidence for finding explicit collusion is operationally undifferentiable from employing the laundry list. Even if the law only extends to explicit collusion, I can introduce as evidence every single item on that laundry list as circumstantial evidence that there was explicit collusion in a given case. You can either apply a per se legal rule for all restrictive practices, or else you are back to something like the laundry list approach as a matter of evidence if not as a matter of doctrine. Indeed, if it is a defense that a practice is ancillary to a lawful objective, clever lawyering can recast almost any business practice you might choose to identify in a way that will afford a plausible defense when the arrangement is ultimately subjected to litigation.

Dam: Something that Baxter said intrigued me. He said that it is true that we might get another aluminum company eventually, but we have to have a fast method of remedying the situation in the meantime and that fast method is an antitrust case. In *Alcoa* you have to remember that Alcoa and the industry completely changed underneath the case. And this leads me back to the symbolic value of antitrust. Most of you don't read Thurman Arnold any more. He stressed the great symbolic value of these opposing armies which fight out the great issue of public policy in the courtroom. Such activity contains a certain amount of social conflict. While these "fights" are going on, however, the industry often changes beneath the cases, though presumably great social tensions will have been released in the interim. This is a large part of what Section 2 antitrust is.

Gellhorn: One further point in this connection is that we should not necessarily be critical of the time it takes to decide a large monopolization case. Maybe ten years is not the ideal time. On the other hand, before you restructure a large industry, I would like some assurance that the decision makers have the facts straight and have some idea of what they're doing. It is not as if we're playing with some minor segment of the economy. So I do not think that the timing aspect, the seemingly endless trials, is something to worry about in these big cases.

Blake: One important point is that economic data and analysis are sufficiently imprecise that other values must necessarily be taken into account in the context of judicial decision-making. Efficiency theory is not well enough developed to provide a manageable framework for factfinding. This leaves room for what I regard as some very basic values implicit in antitrust with respect to distrust of concentrations of power, whether in government or in corporate bureaucracies. How you translate these values into legal rules is more difficult—perhaps as presumptions operative when efficiency considerations are not clear.

Securities-Market Data
and Antitrust Analysis

Brozen: What I've been talking about are abnormal returns in the securities markets. Evidently, there is a capitalization of the superiority of management as it shows up in the securities markets that is worth something in and of itself and that's being capitalized in the securities. I am thus talking about the cumulative return over a 100-month period, the majority of which appeared more than 4 years prior to the acquisition, indicating a superior management team for the firm.

Moreover, the evidence suggests that they pay premiums for the acquired firms. If they were truly in a monopoly position, I don't think they'd have to pay the kinds of premiums that they pay for the acquired firms. That is to say, there wouldn't be competition for the acquired firms.

Eckert: I think the question that is being asked of Brozen is why in the case of the acquisition by a monopoly firm, should there only be one potential acquirer? Why shouldn't there be competition for the field, competition for the right to be a monopolist, that would dissipate this difference in the premium offered for the acquired firm?

Baxter: In a perfect capital-market theory, one assumes that prices always move in discrete steps on the appearance of new information. In order to get the continuing supernormal rates of return that Brozen is talking about, one has to suppose that this set of managers was continually outperforming the expectation of the market about that management. Now that means that the assessment of the market about that management had to be in some sense imperfect.

On the acquired firm side, the story is really quite different. One might ask, why doesn't the market discount the inevitable acquisition? Well, it does; but there's going to be some indeterminate period of time while these assets remain in the hands of inefficient management. Assume there is a 5 percent possibility in any particular month that acquisition will occur in the following month. Well, you discount that stream, and its capitalized value stays below a full capitalization of the acquired firm as of the time when eventual acquisition is at hand. It doesn't stay as low as it would be if there were no chance of acquisition. So long as the acquiring firm is able to pay the premiums that it pays and not earn subnormal rates of return thereafter, it must be realizing an improvement in performance with respect to those acquired assets at least equal to the size of the premium that it paid, which I understand to be Brozen's basic point.

120

Dam: I wanted to be sure I caught everything Baxter was saying. Let me return to the simple logic of Brozen's position. Let's assume an industry with a 50 percent firm, a 20 percent firm, and a bunch of smaller firms. Also, assume that the 20 percent firm is well managed. The 50 percent firm, so Brozen says, is the only one that can pay more for the 20 percent firm. But why is that true? Why wouldn't there be general competition for the control of the 20 percent firm?

Baxter: There will be. All the Gulf and Westerns of the world will be willing to pay the present discounted value of the improved earnings stream that good management can get from the assets of the 20 percent firm. But if you believe in concentration theory at all, the 50 percent firm will be willing to pay an epsilon more, because it is going to buy a larger profit stream for the 50 percent assets it already owns in the industry. Gulf and Western is not in a position to pay this same premium.

Manne: It seems to me there is a little confusion here between efficient and perfect information. The efficient-market hypothesis doesn't suggest that there is complete information. The firms and individuals competing in the market for control of other companies are constantly looking for signals telling where these capital gains may be had. The answer is never immediately evident. Accounting data doesn't tell, and they clearly can't be relying solely on the present stock market price. They've got to seek out new information about an existing management. If somebody sees Gulf and Western make an offer, that's a signal that maybe the target was a company they should have been looking at. So, all the competition would seem to occur in the period after the first offer is made. That is, there's a lot of free riding going in this case, which may or may not be desirable.

Markham: I think the answer is that in order for the monopoly profits to be discounted in the capital market, following the logic of Baxter and Brozen, you have to assume that all those who traded in the stock assumed the monopoly profits would be permanent. If you did that, the capital market reflects and builds into its price a permanent flow of monopoly profits. But this argument empirically falls down, because a sharp estimator will argue that they're making high profits today but competition is going to dissipate those profits. If you make the assumption about good management constantly beating its record, then under those assumed conditions it seems to me Brozen is right. But you have to spell it out in that form.

Baxter: I really don't agree with that argument. Let me suppose that my monopoly profits are going to be dissipated by competition at a rate equal to today's profits over $(1 + r)^n$. Now, I can discount that shrinking stream just as easily as I can discount a constant stream. Therefore, the security price premium that the monopoly firm will carry under a predictable rate of dissipation is a somewhat lower premium than it would carry if permanent monopoly profits were expected. But there will be a premium unless dissipation is instantaneous.

Manne: That's essentially what Markham said. He changed the exogeneous factors, therefore changing the expectations and the stock price. You can disagree with that. Now Schwartz's point was somewhat different. Because, in fact, the profit expectations of the monopoly will show up in the stock price. But it's absolutely indistinguishable from a price change resulting from greater expectations about more firm efficiency. On the other hand, there will be differences in other stocks, and Baxter developed this very well in his paper. And I suspect there's a difference in the effect of these acquisitions on the stock price of competitive firms on the one hand and on acquired firms on the other. For a long time, and I must say in the original article I wrote on this subject in the *Journal of Political Economy* in 1965, I narrowly viewed the impact of a merger on only the acquiring and the acquired companies.[1] This threw some people off who persisted in pursuing that distinction, until we all realized that it was possibly indistinguishable from the effects of monopolizing mergers. However, there are other tests available, and I think that Baxter has advanced the state of the theory in this regard.

Baxter: Yes, if you look at the acquired firm, there's no way of telling why the premium is being paid. But you can tell if you look at the securities prices of competitor firms. This procedure allows you to tell whether the industry is being made more monopolistic or more competitive. Once a merger becomes certain, the security prices of competitor firms, given the change of information, should move in one direction or another. If they move up, the market is telling us that the acquisition had an anticompetitive effect on the industry. That is, competitor security prices should move up in the monopolization case. If the producing assets of the acquired firm are now going to be used more efficiently for larger outputs, competitor security prices should move down. So the sign on the price change of competitor securities distinguishes between these two quite different theories about the reason for the acquisition; the theories are indistinguishable by looking at the securities prices of the merging firms themselves.

Goldberg: But don't conglomerate mergers complicate the use of the securities price approach?

Baxter: First, just because the postmerger firm is a conglomerate does not necessarily mean that either of the premerger firms were conglomerates. Second, even if both merging firms are conglomerates, there will often be competitor firms in the affected market which are not conglomerate. It would not have been very difficult to identify the affected competitors of the Clorox-Proctor Gamble merger, for example. So while conglomerate mergers will complicate the use of this methodology in some instances, it will not do so in all instances.

Note

1. Henry G. Manne, "Mergers and the Market for Corporate Control," *Journal of Political Economy* 73, no. 2 (April 1965):110–120.

Public-Choice Aspects
of Antitrust

Markham: It seems to me that the principle contention between Baxter and Blake is quite clear. Baxter's paper is in the tradition of taking a look at more or less the economic methodology of antitrust and considering that efficiency is clearly, in theory at least, one of the purposes of antitrust. Blake's position is that there are social and political objectives of antitrust, which may not be quantifiable or indeed operational and definable. I think that what I'm going to say, at least tangentially, addresses this apparent conflict.

I think that it's fair to say that Congress clearly is not motivated altogether by considerations of economic efficiency, and one would not expect them to be. All you have to do is look at their miserable record in fiscal policy over the past decade or two for evidence on this score. I think it's also fair to say that judges are not particularly economically sophisticated. But if you look at antitrust, and look at the average, as distinct from the variance about that average, I would submit that antitrust policy is something a little more than a charade. And, indeed, it makes a certain amount of sense. Brozen's data may represent, for example, observations on departures from this average record of antitrust.

But I suspect that the strongest economic arguments that can be made on behalf of antitrust policy relate to overt agreements that circumvent the competitive market, such as horizontal mergers that substantially enhance market share, clear-cut single firm monopoly in the hands of the firm for a long time that can't be explained by technological progress or foresight, and what would be clearly recognized by most people as unfair trade practices. There is a certain underlying rationale of the antitrust laws, and I think some further research would show this rationale in terms of the posture and consistency of antitrust policy.

Siegfried: Baxter's focus, as is common of researchers investigating the gainers and losers from antitrust, is on the functional role of various parties such as consumers, competitors, and the antitrust bar. Another way of looking at who wins and who loses is to compare individuals within the groups of people that have similar functions in the economy. For example, some competitors to an antitrust target firm might have wealthy stockholders and others might have poorer stockholders; some might be big businesses and others might be small businesses. Similar distinctions might be made within the group commonly labeled "consumers": some consumers are wealthy and some are poor; some are Republicans and some

124

are Democrats. Those individuals responsible for the discretionary decisions that determine the enforcement pattern of antitrust (legislators,
enforcement agency staff, and private plaintiffs and their attorneys) might
view the deservedness of different competitors, consumers or other functional parties in distinctly different ways. If this view is accurate, more
variation in the application of the antitrust laws might be explained by looking at characteristics of individuals and firms that vary *within* the groups
that Baxter has identified than by searching for important differences
between the functional groups. For example, if Congress and/or the
enforcement agencies view antitrust as a redistributive program, one might
learn more about patterns of enforcement from knowledge of the wealth or
income levels of the gainers and the losers than from knowledge that they
are consumers, lawyers or small businessmen.

Oi: I am concerned that we are treating antitrust as a homogeneous special
product. As I see it, there are two kinds of antitrust law and enforcement.
One is efficiency-creating laws, and the other is income-redistribution laws.
To treat the two kinds of laws as the same things is like mixing apples and
oranges because we have two very different animals that we are dealing
with. I think that there is ample justification for treating the two types of
laws separately.

Dam: Both the courts and the legislature do make this distinction between
situations in which the property values of small businessmen are affected
and situations in which there are simply expectations that they will be
affected. If you look at legislation having to do with auto dealerships or
service station dealerships, regulation in the energy area having to do with
small refineries, and so forth, what is involved there is the feeling that property values might be destroyed. And that is something that seems to appeal
to people in the realm of political ideas.

On the other hand, I don't see that same disposition with regard to situations in which there isn't a loss of capital value or a loss of an established
position. In the Congress you see the same view with regard to the welfare
area, where the loss of present advantage is viewed as being very important.
For example, it's impossible to change the welfare law if the change would
hurt anybody. There's a law of politics in Congress which seems to say thou
shalt not destroy a present advantage. I don't see the same thing operating
to the same extent in other arenas.

Goldberg: I want to raise a point that Dam made regarding the protection
of gasoline station dealers and car dealers. What is going on here is something that has deeper intellectual and social roots than we've been getting at.
Pigou and Dicey note that the same sort of issues arose in the nineteenth-

century English land law.[1,2] Legislation giving seniority to labor provides another example. Very similar arrangements show up in most European countries. There's something going on here that is not simply a matter of small business being protected. I think that there is something deeper going on than just simply a naive political effort to protect these particularly powerful interest groups. The same phenomenon recurs too often in too many different contexts.

Dam: I would like to label what Goldberg is talking about, for the purpose of discussion, a social property right that the courts and the legislatures are recognizing.

Goldberg: I think the gasoline-dealer case particularly is an area where the issue is protecting the existing dealers from termination because of the changes in the industry that have taken place since 1973. I gather the old contracts essentially made it very, very difficult for the oil companies to raise rents to their dealer tenants, and there were all sorts of advantages to getting rid of the network small dealers that had been built up. One way for the dealers to protect themselves in this situation was to pass a law prohibiting oil companies from owning and operating stations.

Manne: I don't want to let Ken Dam get a concept like "social property rights" on the books without entering a demurrer to it. I don't know how to define it or cope with it, and I don't think they exist. He must have something else in mind.

Dam: There is a large amount of litigation in this area leading from contract to status. Although you can make important legal distinctions here, in the minds of many people who think about it, particularly those who don't think about it very carefully, dealerships are status arrangements that ought to be protected, whether from competition from the outside (which is viewed as something that the manufacturer does to punish the dealer by putting in another dealer in competition with him) or from outright termination. It boils down to the same thing from the standpoint of the existing dealer, and looks the same way, smells the same way, from the standpoint of the legislature or the court.

Manne: But surely you don't need a concept like "social property rights" to describe the redistribution of individual property rights. If you change the property rights, you have a wealth redistribution.

Dam: All I intended by the notion of, let me call them status- rather than social property rights if you prefer, was to distinguish this particular idea of property rights from the idea that we've used in the property-rights litera-ture. I am talking about the creation by law of rights in things which previ-ously were governed by nonexclusive arrangements. One of the unfortunate aspects of this movement in law and legislation is that it involves protection against competition, mostly that kind of informal competition which takes the form of the manufacturer deciding that the distributor isn't being effi-cient and therefore he replaces him. But these cases represent a kind of status in which people have invested, and they have an expectation that is legitimate and therefore is entitled to protection by the courts or by legisla-tion.

Williamson: I would like to ask a question about this notion as to the legiti-macy of expectations. It seems to me that the error arises over failure to examine the whole contracting process as a system. When you make the ori-ginal contract, certain values are associated with that agreement. Fran-chisees are not anxious to pay large capital sums for their original arrange-ments. Once they have the franchise in place, they'd like to have it redefined and have the terms legitimized to their advantage.

Baxter: I understand exactly what Dam is saying. He's talking about the perceptions of legislators in general. Williamson is saying those perceptions are in fact wrong in the dynamic sense, because after the legal rules are changed, the contracts negotiated between the parties will change in various ways in addition to the way required by the rule change. And I say yes, of course, that's what we've discovered in rent control and a lot of other situa-tions. But this is one of the respects in which I think a society can system-atically err over a long period of time before it collectively becomes aware of the error. I agree completely that there is a total misconception on the part of legislatures and courts in general that they are helping the small enterprises when they disable them from entering into certain kinds of agreements.

Graglia: I was struck by Dam's remark that you can explain cases like the IBM case as a catharsis, a relieving of public passions that might otherwise explode in some other direction. It seemed to me that the public passions against IBM prior to the case were well under control. There seemed not to be much pressure in that direction, but since the case, it seems there has been some such pressure. Since the case, you have things at my university like the LBJ School of Public Affairs where they hold seminars on the IBM case and professors get up and explain to the students in some detail what a beastly company this is. Now a lot of passion comes out of that, and the students come marching out of those discussions saying "Down with IBM." This passion didn't exist before.

I had a student in an antitrust seminar from Japan. At several points during the course of the seminar, he would say to me. "You say that you're speaking candidly, openly, and I think you are candid. Now I want you to tell me the real reason the government is bringing the IBM case." And I would say, "I'll be darned if I can tell you, or at least easily." And he says, "Oh, you're part of it too." Here's a guy from Japan where the government does everything it can to help the computer industry, and then there is this "pretense" going on in the United States that the United States is trying to stop IBM. He just can't believe it.

Markham: I'd like to say a few words about the business of constituency. I think one could very easily use the constituency hypothesis and test it in the case of antitrust exemptions. But it may very well be when you get to something like the Sherman Act or Section 7 of the Clayton Act that the relevant model might very well be something like rivalrous activity for power. The whole notion of a constituency is that in the political sense there are sufficient numbers of people out there to make it worthwhile for politicians to respond to them. It may very well be that the rivalry of power model would explain a good deal more in that politicians like to exercise power. After all, this is one of the objectives of seeking office, to exercise tremendous power. Large corporations are viewed as arising in the form of trusts, and they pose something of a threat to that power. And if you put yourself in that kind of political world, you have very little to lose by voting for the Sherman Act. And that's basically why all but one senator voted for it.

This hypothesis takes on a little more realism when you get to the present proposals for antitrust reform or for modifications of antitrust laws. I think that Senator Kennedy does view a constituency when he thinks in terms of those bills that he's gone for, which were designed to cut down the vertical integration of oil companies, because there is a very large oil-consuming group in the polity. He can't get at OPEC to save his neck, and so he throws in a lot of bills that appeal to oil consumers. So I think that the rivalrous power model makes a lot more sense in analyzing antitrust constituencies.

Graglia: Since the Sherman Act seems to say very little, it's easy to see why it was virtually unopposed. When its applications have hurt somebody, then you get opposition. There is a very similar example if you look at the Congress and the issue of the Equal Rights Amendment. Who would vote against equality for women? However, when the question arises in a specific context, should women be drafted, should there be distinctions in athletic appropriations, and so on, you find great conflict. Now you've got real issues.

This leads me to a related question, which I think Dam raised. Namely, what is the constituency of the Supreme Court? Here, you have a phenomenon of this institution behaving in a way that apparently hurts a lot of people, and yet nothing can be done. Nothing comes even close to being done. And it seems to me that this is something that requires some real explanation. Now part of the answer is that people don't want to "fiddle with the Constitution," and such beliefs are very strong.

Morgan: One of the things that has intrigued me about this whole area is why the antitrust laws began not as a regulatory system, such as the Interstate Commerce Act or other statutes passed around that time, but rather as a criminal provision, as an attack on people who were perceived to be criminals.

It seems to me that one of the reasons we get the policies we do is because of the cost of providing the public adequate information to allow them to make entirely rational decisions. Policies tend to be made in directions that are influenced by how cheap it is to acquire information, or how much information appears to be available at a given point of time. This may lead to systematic errors in policies based upon the fact that people simply are not going to take the time to learn all there is to learn about the factors that ought to go into a decision.

I suggest that to a great extent the media is the villain. If you call a press conference to announce that you are going to get a different level of efficiency in the economy by changing a legal rule in a particular way, you are going to be talking to an empty hall. Nobody is going to come, and nobody is going to report what you say. If you announce that the oil company executives are getting rich or that the oil companies are the villains, you'll get a substantial amount of public attention.

I suggest that it is relatively easy for people to understand and characterize villains but relatively difficult for people to understand questions about economic efficiency. Our task then becomes to figure out a cost-effective way of providing alternative understandings and information for the public that can be translated into the policies that we think will lead to better long-run results.

Notes

1. A.C. Pigou, *The Economics of Welfare,* 4th ed. (London: Macmillan & Co., 1932).

2. A.V. Dicey, *Law and Public Opinion in England* (London: Macmillan & Co., 1963).

Antitrust as a Substitute for Socialism

Manne: May I suggest that we go to a point that Dewey has made, I believe now in print, a notion that we have antitrust because there is a fear of what the alternative would be if we didn't have it.

Dewey: When it comes to antitrust matters, I'm now totally schizophrenic Over the years I have come to the conclusion that there is no sound case grounded in economic welfare for antitrust. Here, I'd take a stand with Brozen and say that antitrust comes at a cost. I'm not sure, but I'm beginning to think that the costs are fairly high, perhaps even higher than Brozen indicates. One important cost of antitrust is very well concealed, namely, the generation of a great deal of excess capacity throughout the economy—excess capacity that could be eliminated by price wars, mergers, and cartels. I think that this cost is very well concealed, because it does not create any noticeable political discontent.

I also happen to feel, from reading the history of antitrust, that the desire to maximize welfare, or merely to increase economic welfare, has been a very minor goal of the policy. Here I'm almost inclined to introduce a marriage theory of research on antitrust. Baxter married a statistician, so he runs regressions. I married an English socialist and acquired a socialist daughter. So I fight ideological battles almost daily.

And, of course, in economic policy the really big battle is between people who wish to expand the public sector at the expense of the private sector and people who are endeavoring to resist this trend. Viewed in this context, I think that antitrust is a profoundly important policy. I would cite de Tocqueville to Yale Brozen on this point. De Tocqueville was very contemptuous of the French middle classes of his day on the ground that they hadn't learned from experience. The French Revolution, he held, should have taught them the utility of religion, if not its truth. I would suggest that events in the rest of the world should have taught Yale the utility of antitrust, if not its truth.

I have suggested elsewhere that to make a good case for antitrust in this country one must view it as substitute for socialism. For considered as a part of the defensive strategy of the existing order, antitrust makes a great deal of sense. To date its costs have not been very high, it generates political support, and it commends itself to a wide range of opinion.

Why does antitrust persist? I think we can answer this question pretty well by noting that it has obviously acquired momentum and that there's a tendency to stick with any economic policy unless there's very strong persuasive evidence that it is not working. To me the fascinating question is how antitrust became respectable because in 1890 it was not a respectable policy. It was a piece of populist rhetoric that went through Congress with virtually no opposition. Yet it was almost totally condemned or ignored by leading lawyers and economists of that era. Then somehow over the years it has become a sacred cow in American politics.

When I took a course in the methodology of history, I was told that "inevitable" was the favorite word of a bad historian and to be avoided in so far as possible. But there is surely something inevitable about antitrust policy in this country. That is, if you're not going the socialist route and if you can't accept a complete laissez-faire philosophy, what do you do? Antitrust has fairly low apparent costs, and it does produce rather striking visible results. There's no doubt that the structure of the economy as reflected in concentration ratios would be radically different in the absence of an antitrust policy. The absence of extensive cartelization in this country can be traced directly to antitrust policy. Consider all the ill-advised legislation presently being proposed for the oil industry. If we nationalize oil, that would be serious. A few divestiture decrees inflicted on the oil industry would not be all that significant.

Markham: May I add a footnote to this? There is some corroboration to what Dewey said. I don't know how many of you have read the proceedings of the American Economic Association in 1886. It's not the most inspiring literature in the world, but it does shed some light on this issue. The big debate among Adams, Ely, and the men of that day was about the new antitrust legislation that was offered in the Senate, and whether you wouldn't accomplish much more through the socialization of industry. So Dewey's argument has historical precedent.

Graglia: When I hear discussion about the symbolic value of antitrust or antitrust as a barrier to the coming of socialism in this country, I can't help but hear it with a great deal of skepticism. Perhaps such arguments come from people who have devoted themselves to a particular subject, and who indulge themselves in a very natural assumption that their subject is very important. As I heard Dewey state the "prevents socialism" idea, however, I thought that he put it in a form that made it have at least some credibility, namely that without antitrust we would have presumably unlimited cartelization and mergers. If this took place, in times of perhaps unhappy economic performance, there would certainly be greater ease in government taking over the resulting companies. I am willing to concede that there might be something to that.

Crawford: My comment is in response to Dewey's view that antitrust is a substitute for socialism. When we think about the competitive organization of society, we emphasize its efficiencies but not its distributional effects on wealth. In the competitive process there are winners and losers, and if those winners and losers align themselves on the basis of talent we can converge over time to a consistent set of losers. Being a loser tends to generate anger and disenchantment with the competitive system. However, for lotteries with independent outcomes, this distributional effect is not present. Also, we look at competition in sports as something delightful precisely because there is a systematic restart every year which makes consistent winning difficult. Thus we don't get the same set of losers over time. Random antitrust enforcement can accomplish the same thing. Randomly prosecuting a set of winners each time does not encourage a consistent set of losers with incentives to disrupt the system.

Dewey: Antitrust does work to dampen down political passions, in a number of ways, but I am not happy with the term *symbolic value.* Antitrust, whatever its virtues or vices, has prevented the cartelization of the economy and substantially reduced concentration ratios across the board. I am also prepared to accept that these achievements have a cost. On balance, they have probably reduced economic welfare, not increased it. But I think that there may be a substantial economic payoff, if the goal is to prevent the encroachment of the public sector on the private sector, from these achievements of antitrust.

Blake: If it were not for antitrust, there would surely have been even more intrusive government intervention in regulating the economy. I agree with Dewey that antitrust is not entirely symbolic, but I suspect it's partly symbolic.

Baxter: For these symbolic purposes wouldn't it be enough if we had basically the horizontal approach? Wouldn't these purposes be satisfied by an anti-cartel and anti-horizontal-merger rule? Is it really necessary to have a prohibition against the nonproportionate distribution of advertising posters?

Dam: I'm puzzled here. I thought it startling that Blake would say that Dewey's explanation was similar to his. If I think of the various problem areas of antitrust, and if I think of Blake's small-business, Jeffersonian-Democracy model, I end up with only a single area in which the two explanations cover the same activities, and that is the conglomerate merger area. And even there I am skeptical because Dewey's rules would lead us to say that we need rules against cartelization and concentration, because otherwise you would get a very concentrated economy and probably nationalization. Yet cartelization is very good for small business, and the opportunity to sell out to one's competitors is very good for the small entrepreneur.

Schwartz: It seems to me that there's a problem with Dewey's arguments. Presumably, we've got a market for legislation here, and we have to specify what is being brought. Among the many problems, I have with Dewey's argument is that it is stated in terms of the discrete alternatives of socialism or antitrust. It seems to me that the government can supply a wide variety of products to cater to these tastes, whatever they are. We have restrictions on international trade, subsidies, tax law, limitations on the professions, and so on, and it seems to me that you have to identify the antitrust laws as supplying products which a believable group of demanders are demanding through the political system The alternative to socialism argument doesn't persuade me because the people who want what you're saying are not getting it.

Manne: If I may interject my own observation here, I would point out the possible countervailing theory, which would, I suspect, have as much empirical support as Donald Dewey's, that is, the longer a country has antitrust laws on its books, the closer it moves to socialism.

Markham: I'd agree with everything that Dewey says, but I don't think that relieves one of taking a look at what the real objectives of antitrust policy are. You can have alternative antitrust policies that would still serve as a symbol. It could be a pure symbol in the sense that I'm told that one Virginia politician during the women's suffragette movement argued that we really must let women vote as much as they want, only we must not count them. This would be purely symbolic. But I think that there is still an awful lot to be said on the issue of whether or not antitrust is to be directed by economics toward efficiency.

Comparisons with
Other Countries

Kitch: It may be useful to ask some comparative questions. Closely related to any comparative questions is an ambiguity as to what antitrust is and what rules it includes. The basic question that we have to ask is whether the phenomenon we're trying to explain is largely or exclusively American, largely or exclusively twentieth century, or whether we are trying to explain a phenomenon which we see occurring in many market economies. There is a lot of expertise here about the extent to which the American arrangements can be viewed as unique or not. I have a rough impression that they were unique until after World War II, and then there was a period of antitrust imperialism during which our antitrust statutes were exported to or emulated by other countries.

Williamson: I think that what you say was true in Germany and Japan, although I suspect that antitrust was implemented in a more serious way in Germany than in Japan. I think there's also an interesting comparative difference in terms of what goes on in industrial organization research between the United States and Europe. I would judge that European scholars in this area are doing essentially industrial organization research that was going on in the United States back in the mid-1960s. It's essentially studies of the structure-conduct-performance type, and to the extent that it has an impact on what happens in the enforcement sphere, I would imagine some of the strains that we were talking about earlier will be appearing there. They simply don't seem to have a keen appreciation for efficiency, in all its various manifestations, as a part of their research studies.

Blake: I'm not sure that there is very much to be learned from comparisons with foreign counterparts of antitrust. The differences between foreign antitrust regimes and ours are great. For example, in Latin America, where you find some antitrust laws that look something like ours, they are almost invariably used to defend domestic industry against foreign intruders. And in the case of Germany and Japan, I doubt that you'd find very much basis for support of the theory that small business is an important constituency of antitrust.

Manne: How about the interests of public officials in these things? Certainly, the enforcement techniques of antitrust in Western Europe don't rely in any sense on the private bar.

Markham: I would like to say a few words about the question of the uniqueness of U.S. antitrust policy. Most of the Western European countries would tell you that antitrust, where you think in terms of maintaining competitive structures, is simply not a feasible alternative for those countries. For one thing, their economies are simply too small. If you have any economies of scale at all, you're going to end up with an industrial base that is concentrated. For example, you couldn't think in terms of really breaking up the automobile companies in Germany, where you have essentially two companies. Secondly, because of the small-economy setting, there is greater use of liberalization of trade as a means of controlling competition.

However, when you start looking at the six-nation European Economic Community, it looks as though, when you put these six countries together, you have something on the order of the United States economy. It does make a certain amount of sense at this juncture to think of an antitrust policy like our own, but quite different from our own in terms of how it is administered.

Schwartz: I would just like to point out that the Common Market is ahead of us in the jurisprudence of efficiency enhancement by contract. That's for two reasons. First, their equivalent of Section 1 requires a rule of reason, which implicates efficiency analysis. Second, because of national problems as they perceive them, mergers are difficult. Cooperation among enterprises thus takes the form of contract. So they have been ahead of us in making essentially free-rider arguments for things like market division among firms selling common products.

The Private Bar and
Antitrust Policy

Schwartz: I have been following with a lot of interest a funny kind of political rivalry, and that's the rivalry to get the job of enforcing the antitrust laws. You obviously have the Justice Department and the Federal Trade Commission in this competition. But you also have the state attorneys general, you've got direct purchasers, and you've got private lawyers, and these groups have been extremely active in carrying on a political rivalry. The only problem is that every model that I apply to the outcome produces the wrong result, and I was just going to report the single piece of empirical work that I did in this area. I said to myself that if *Illinois Brick* gets overruled and you have suits by consumers, it will increase the cost of antitrust enforcement substantially. And, therefore, I would suppose that antitrust enforcement would be less efficient, and its deterrent effect would be decreased. This is my model, and there the likely antitrust defendants would be great supporters of the bill to overturn *Illinois Brick*. This is because they would then be able to pursue monopoly profits and be less concerned about antitrust enforcement. However, the business community appears to be pursuing the public interest in this case, and my empirical work suggests that the wrong people were showing up and saying the wrong things at the hearings. All the big defendants were saying that you will be less able to zing us if you pass this bill. Therefore, don't pass it. What is the model, if you will, of this sort of "public-interest" behavior?

Baxter: I have no difficulty in giving you my explanation of this. These firms are not really concerned about having to disgorge anything that they regard as monopoly profits. The expenses of litigating a major antitrust case are large. The modest cases run to over $1 million a year. They can easily run to $5 million a year. So it seems to me that what you see is firms rebelling against what they see as an enormous escalation in the cost of trying these cases.

Schwartz: But the model they advance is that since those additional costs will be largely born by plaintiffs, the consequence will be that they will have fewer such suits to bring. That's the argument they make in testimony.

Baxter: But that's because the people who listen to those arguments believe in Dewey's symbolism, which requires that they believe, or appear to believe, in the efficacy of the antitrust laws for preventing monopoly pricing. And if one puts oneself in that frame of mind, then one dares not talk about weakening the deterrent effect of this marvelous body of law. That's what sells, but it's not the motivating force for the business firms. They are concerned about an enormous increase in the costs of trying these crazy suits. Now the fact that the plaintiff's expenses are also increased is largely irrelevant, because when you lose one of these things, you wind up paying their expenses too.

Schwartz: But if I understand your point then, you are saying that the net consequence of overturning *Illinois Brick* would be to increase the deterrent effect, because the increased costs of litigating the additional issues that would be implicated would be placed sufficiently upon defendants as to override any possible deterrent effect on the bringing of suits because of the increased costs of plaintiffs.

Baxter: That's what I think the reality is. Now, what you take the "deterrent effect" of the antitrust law to be, of course, gets fairly critical here. The primary deterrent effect of the antitrust law, as far as I am able to observe it, is to deter unusual and strong competitive moves of a variety of kinds. Reorganizing your distribution system, cutting of this shnook in Kalamazoo who isn't doing a good job for you, making an acquisition of another company whose assets exhibit high complementarity to your own, disciplining your sales force better, these are the types of actions that antitrust deters. Some of these actions are probably desirable things, but many of them are obviously undesirable. What the balance represents is an open question.

Schwartz: So to summarize the position of the efficiency-oriented witnesses, the consequence of the reversal of *Illinois Brick* would be to increase the deterrent effect of antitrust laws. But since the antitrust laws are in large part perverse, the consequences will be negative, but we can't say that to Congress. So what we do is misstate the deterrent effect in order to save the world from antitrust.

Baxter: Right on the nose.

Schwartz: Well, I tend to disagree with you on this. The assumption is that fewer enforcement proceedings will be brought, because you have made litigation more costly. They will say that the possible increase in the number of potential plaintiffs will be more than outweighed by the fact that litigation will be costly. That is the party-line opposition to the overturning of *Illinois Brick*. What is curious to me is that the people who are saying this would be the principal people harmed by such legislation. Therefore, the thing that has struck me is they are testifying against their own self-interest. They are testifying for efficiency in enforcement, where if the enforcement is more efficient, they will be the losers.

Calvani: I'm reminded that each year when the Robinson-Patman Committee of the American Bar Association gets together to talk about legislation, their basic line is let's support the Robinson-Patman Act because it supports us. If you begin looking at gainers and losers of antitrust litigation, it seems to me that one of the clearly identifiable gainers is the antitrust bar. While it may be confusing to look at *Illinois Brick* from the defense perspective, if you look at it from the point of view of the plaintiff's lawyers, I think it's more instructive. At first it appears confusing because you've got this group of plaintiff attorneys who are appearing at the congressional hearings, and they take different positions. Some of them support reversal, and some of them do not. I think Posner was originally puzzled by this. But he recently told me that he had gone through and categorized these plaintiff attorneys. It was very interesting to find out that the plaintiff attorneys who were calling for reversal represented on balance a different class of plaintiffs than the ones who were opposing it. You had one group of plaintiff attorneys who represented people who would be benefited by passing the law, and another group of plaintiff attorneys who would not be benefited by passing the law. And it's not surprising that these two groups of plaintiff attorneys took radically different perspectives. So I think you learn something by looking at the behavior of plaintiffs attorneys in the *Illinois Brick* decision.

Kitch: I think that's very important. If you look at who the plaintiffs' lawyers were who were opposed to the *Illinois Brick* legislation, you realize that their time is so valuable in settling cases that they don't want to have situations in which settlement is more complicated. That's how I interpret their testimony, and that's how I think, in fact, their practice works. It is not so much who they represent. It is how they conduct their practice.

Morgan: This raises what I believe to be the factually accurate point that attorneys' fees in antitrust cases are paid over and above the judgment, not as a part of the judgment. So we're not talking about contingent fees in the classic sense, where the plaintiff winds up directly paying. We're talking about an add-on which is frequently calculated in relation to the amount recovered. I understand that the basis of calculation is changing to some extent now, but we're still talking about an add-on figure. Whether you win or lose the case or settlement, you get attorneys' fees. This goes to Kitch's point. If you lose an ordinary case, you don't get attorneys' fees.

I can imagine someone testifying that if you up the ante for private plaintiffs (because you've increased plaintiffs' costs) as a result of overturning *Illinois Brick,* you will decrease the total number of plaintiffs' suits, at least in theory. But the person could maintain that position with a straight face and still be very disturbed about overturning *Illinois Brick,* because the cases that would be brought, if they are brought, will be likely to be for a substantially higher amount than the increased costs of litigation.

Dam: I think Morgan is on the right track here. When one talks about these cases, it's fairly important to distinguish on the plaintiff's side between the plaintiff's attorney and the plaintiff. It's important to look at what the fee arrangements are. It's also important to recognize that although there might be an interest of defendants as a class, when you get to a particular case, the defendant may have a particular interest that is different from the interest of the defendants as a class. For example, I believe that there are far more settlements than most people realize, that take the form of settling with the plaintiff's attorney rather than with the plaintiff. I believe a very large number of settlements take the form of paying the plaintiffs legal expenses, which may include hourly charges, but certainly will include all the out-of-pocket expenses. On the other hand, a lawyer can file a complaint to make it clear to the defendant that the case might turn into a class-action litigation, in which event even a class-action may be settled without any supervision by the court if it's not class action yet. And there are very few corporate defendants who are really willing to fight, if they can get out of the litigation for a relatively small amount of money. So that is why I say that plaintiff's counsels are in the business of settling cases and not in the business of litigating suits.

Kitch: In looking at the data on case-bringing activity, everything appears consistent with the Dewey hypothesis, except for the shift in the trend line in private cases which have now risen to the level where the phenomenon is large enough to have macrosocial consequences. My understanding of this rise in private litigation is that it is due to the courts' increased willingness to be receptive to private cases and to a change in the class-action rule. Of these two, the latter effect seems more significant than the first. And this generates the question as to what happened to get this change in trend around 1960? Part of the explanation could be the change in the location of rule-making power in 1939, but it took time for the bar to learn how to manipulate the rule-making power in a way which generates a shift in trends favorable to the input of services from the bar. That's not such an easy thing to do. You have to acquire a certain amount of expertise, and somewhere in the 1960s the bar learned how to capture this process. At this point the rule started to make a difference. Now there are signs of counterreaction. There are recent rule changes that the Congress has balked at. But these things take a long time to work themselves out, and we will have to wait to see if a new change of trend actually occurs.

Dam: In the *Caucasian Chalk Circle,* a play by Bertolt Brecht, the judge asks one of the litigants for a bribe, and somebody standing by expresses shock. The judge responds, however, "Oh you shouldn't worry about that, the only way I can be unbiased in a case is to accept money from both sides." Judges may also benefit from decision-making by indulging their tastes without actually being biased in a particular case. The *Bigelow* decision and the judicial interpretation of the class action rule, Rule 23, may reflect the indulgence of a judicial taste. Similarly, in a vast number of decisions during the 1960s having to do with procedural questions, the Supreme Court made it much easier for plaintiffs to litigate and to win. In each instance decisions were taken by judges who are on fixed incomes, and who therefore are indulging their personal tastes and not having to bear any of the costs. I don't think that the class action rules were some sort of manipulation by the private bar that saw what a bonanza they would be. It was quite a surprise to everyone concerned just what a vast expansion of litigation occurred. One of the great puzzles here is how these tremendous changes with great consequences occur largely without recognition at the time of what their vast significance is. It isn't that there is persistent error. It is that people don't think enough about and don't have any incentive to predict future consequences. It is the uncertainty as to the future that is interesting, and one doesn't need a persistent error hypothesis to explain judicial behavior. This is somewhat related to the earlier discussion about Congressmen. Since nobody seems to know who the winners and losers will be or the winners and losers aren't sufficiently well organized to bring it to the legislator's attention in a forceful way, why shouldn't the legislator vote for the prevailing ideology?

Goldberg: The point I want to make is related to the question of why the big jump in the 1960s in private litigation. I think it is true that both of the procedural reforms that have been mentioned are important. There is also another important aspect of this development—the *Schwinn* decision. This decision created for at least a ten-year period a very large class of new plaintiffs, namely terminated dealers. And that's where a very large share of the cases came from. It was not strictly a procedural change, but to some extent a real substantive change.

Compensation and
Antitrust Policy

Schwartz: I think that this is part of a much more general phenomenon than antitrust that I have puzzled about a good deal. In the United States you have a wedding of two ideas, and as far as I know, it is an exclusive marriage and doesn't exist anywhere else in the world. You have taken a very wide range of economic regulation, and you have wedded that to the notion of private enforcement. Indeed, many economists are attracted to the concept of competition in enforcement. It turns out not to be a very good market, I think, but they like the idea of people out there competing. Moreover, if you read the antitrust enforcement discussion in Congress and treat it seriously, there is a notion that is constantly asserted that compensation is an independently desirable goal. Indeed, the political parties are now split in antitrust. The Republicans are prodeterrent, and Democrats are pro-compensation. This is different than redistribution. The idea is that it is better to get the money back in the hands of the person overcharged. Whether compensation has a real social value or whether this is a case of the private bar cynically incorporating an idea to their advantage, I don't know. But if you did an empirical test of how often a word is mentioned in something like the overturning of *Illinois Brick,* the notion of compensation as an independently desirable objective comes up very often. The notion of redressing grievances and not only preventing inefficiency is thus gaining currency in the antitrust area.

Markham: Why not pay compensation if people are injured by an illegal course of conduct?

Schwartz: Well you know the classic answer to that. The classic answer is that identifying who was hurt and how much each individual was hurt is a very costly exercise, probably not worth engaging in. I gather, for example, that Blake thinks it is worth engaging in.

Blake: I think that I do.

Graglia: It seems to me that Blake is on very strong ground in some of his ideas about the various kinds of hard-to-specify, emotional-type satisfactions served by antitrust. These things can be very nebulous, but the idea of compensation seems much less so since people have been injured by behavior thought to be wrongful. Of course, one might say as an economist that finding those people and compensating them is not worth the cost, but that just doesn't seem persuasive to most people in that context.

Schwartz: This may be one of the cases where ideas are mattering. Because if you break the idea of compensation down, the likely gains and losses of individuals is really a lousy buy, and it gets you into the whole incidence analysis question. If you are really going to do compensation, you are going to have to trace out all these effects.

Dam: Well, most lawyers don't think that you have to trace out all the effects. They say that economists just want to do too much with rationalism. As lawyers, we have not figured out the world that well, and we are not yet all convinced that economists have done so. But when we have figured out that somebody is hurt by wrongful actions and we can find some way to compensate him, we think that we ought to do it.

Schwartz: Even if you compensate them too much? And there are lots of people you don't compensate, and it is largely random as to whom you do compensate. It seems to me that there are serious operational problems with a policy of compensation for antitrust harm.

Developments in State
Antitrust Activities

Morgan: I hesitate to introduce a new problem or research topic at this late stage. But I want to pick up on a point that Tollison made earlier, and that is that it is easy for us to think of the Sherman Act as having been adopted almost a hundred years ago and conclude that the great changes have only come in subsequent litigation. However, the Sherman Act is being re-adopted year after year in many states.

I think it was 1967 that Illinois adopted a state antitrust statute that essentially picks up, lock, stock, and barrel, except for the merger provisions, the federal antitrust law. There is also a model state antitrust statute which, as I understand it, is being adopted in some form and with some changes in a variety of states across the country.

Who is behind those statutes? Who is taking out the parts that they're not adopting? I don't know the answer to these questions, other than to observe in Illinois that I think what happened was that the legislature was basically ignorant of the substance of what it was adopting. It had heard that the Sherman Act was a good thing, and therefore passed it. Also, the bar association had a committee which was established to write the law and which explained it in great detail.

I suggest, then, that we are looking at a situation in which there is a lot of activity at the state legislative level, although not necessarily at the congressional level, and that there may well be some fruitful opportunity for research at this level.

Day: As a matter of fact, I am currently chairman of the Committee for the Uniform State Antitrust Act. Oddly enough, it took a long time for the National Conference of Commissioners on Uniform State Laws to finally adopt a uniform antitrust act for the states. And there was a great deal of debate and give and take at the national conferences, which were composed of widely divergent views of people from the various states. The Uniform Act is pretty much the Sherman Act, so that one might ask what's the big deal about it, why all the fuss? The big deal in my opinion is what was left out, not what was put in. The Act went through various drafts, and at one time it contained a long laundry list of things that were to be per se illegal. I argued against this approach, and I didn't want to include the Clayton Act Sections 2, 3, 7, and 8. I was concerned about what might happen if all these states start getting into antitrust activity and mess it up worse than the private plaintiffs. What we didn't want, for example, is for the state attorneys general to bring politics into the enforcement of these laws. We feared

143

such things happening as a merger in a small town challenged on the incipiency test of Clayton Act Section 7. We didn't want this to happen, so we intentionally left the Clayton Act out. What we wanted to do was to codify essentially the Sherman Act. We didn't want every little restraint of trade, reasonable as well as unreasonable, attacked in the state courts.

Consider what is happening presently in South Carolina, where the judges from our State Supreme Court brag that they never even heard of antitrust cases or never saw one in all the time that they have been practicing. Suddenly, we have the Congress granting money to the attorneys general of the states, including South Carolina where they now establish a special section for antitrust. South Carolina, and I am just using this as an example for it is also true in other states, has not only a little Sherman Act, but a little Federal Trade Commission Act which gives a right to private treble damages and embodies a very lenient proof of damages. This has not been widely discovered yet by the private bar, but it is being discovered. There is a combination of factors that I think we all ought to be aware of that really gives me a cause to pause and be frightened. In addition to these state statutes with private treble damages, attorneys' fees, and so on, South Carolina now has a whole new section in the attorney general's office just looking for a way to justify its existence. When you put all these things together, you don't have to be too brilliant to see the possibilities here. I foresee a real growth in antitrust activity not only in South Carolina but in other states. In addition, the costs of enforcement might shift very drastically and very suddenly because of a very active trial bar suddenly bringing actions on the local level in small towns, against small businesses. I would like to see the antitrust laws, if we are going to have private actions, to be limited to per se types of conspiracies, restraints of trade, and unfair trade practices of the traditional kind.

I would also like to say that the use of the antitrust laws may be a reasonable alternative to what could be worse. The development of the Uniform State Antitrust Act is consistent with this view. Why promote the Uniform State Antitrust Law if I don't want the states getting involved in this? The answer is, considering the alternatives, what we did is a lesser evil. We came up with an antitrust law which is much less harmful, I think, than what could have happened and what is happening in some of the states. Unfortunately, some states do not view the Uniform Act as strong enough, and they're moving toward treating every little local restraint as a subject for antitrust action. If the antitrust laws are carried too far in their enforcement at the local level, the result could be antitrust as something worse than the alternatives.

Let me give you one example, The *Royal Drug* case. The question was whether Blue Cross is exempt in setting prices they pay for drugs for their insurance clients. On that point, the Supreme Court said no, they are not exempt, so that an antitrust case could be brought. But the Department of Justice filed a brief, which was noted in a footnote to the opinion, that suggested that even though such activity was subject to the antitrust laws, this particular kind of arrangement probably was not a violation. What I get out of this is that the Department of Justice would not bring that suit. This demonstrates a point. The Department of Justice wouldn't "over-enforce" the antitrust laws, but private plaintiffs will. I don't know what the court is going to say in this case, but I think that based on precedent there is support for the theory of a conspiracy to fix prices.

Now, what does all this mean? Senator Kennedy, a stong antitrust enforcer, might say that whenever Blue Cross or other insurance companies get contracts for their clients with pharmacies, nursing homes, hospitals, and doctors, to fix or limit prices, such actions are all illegal under the antitrust law. On the other hand, Senator Kennedy has said that the cost of medical care is increasing at an alarming rate, and, therefore, we ought to nationalize medicine. And here may be a case where an over-enforcement of the antitrust laws might result in something which is worse—excessive antitrust enforcement, leading to higher costs, resulting in nationalized medicine. That sort of completes the picture of what I think we are talking about.

Adams: Well, I've had a little recent experience with proposed antitrust legislation here in Florida. I've talked to some legislators, and they don't seem to have strong feelings. As Morgan suggested, they feel that any progressive state must have an antitrust law. We don't have one, so we should go ahead and pass one. The people who seem to be really pressing for an antitrust law in Florida are members of the antitrust section of the Bar. They are generally plaintiffs' attorneys, who are aligned with an attorney general, who, I think, has his own interest in promoting an antitrust act. I think there is a perception among plaintiffs' attorneys that they will fare better in state courts than they do in federal courts because the federal courts are beginning to gain a little more experience and maturity in this area. As a result they are losing cases they formerly might have won. They may feel that if a new forum is made available where the judges have not had very much experience, they will end up being able to get better results.

Galvani: It seems to me that if you look at the real genesis of state antitrust activity, it occurred about three years ago when a significant amount of money was distributed to state antitrust agencies. It's at the same time that you see the National Association of State Attorneys General become a very effective lobby in Congress for antitrust "reform." Just drawing on our experiences in the state of Tennessee, where two years ago we had no antitrust division with no budget, today they have gone from $0 to $400,000 a year. That's going to be a tremendous growth industry, and I think it relates to the natural bureaucratic proclivities of state antitrust officials. I really see this as relating to the bureaucracy element of the Baxter paper.

About the Contributors

William F. Baxter is William Benjamin Scott and Luna M. Scott Professor at the Stanford Law School. He received the A.B. and J.D. degrees from Stanford University. He has been a visiting professor at Yale and a Fellow at the Center for Advanced Studies in Behavioral Sciences. His specialties are antitrust, law and social science, regulated industries, administrative law, and federal jurisdiction.

Harlan M. Blake is professor in the Columbia University School of Law. He received the B.A., M.A., and J.D. degrees from the University of Chicago. Besides teaching at Columbia, Professor Blake has taught at the University of Minnesota. He was director of the European Common Market antitrust project for five years. He specializes in antitrust, comparative economic law, law and economic development, trade regulation, and law and economics.

Yale Brozen is professor at the University of Chicago Graduate School of Business. He received the Ph.D. from the University of Chicago. He has taught at the University of Minnesota and at Northwestern University. Professor Brozen has published extensively in the fields of antitrust and economic regulation.

Kenneth W. Dam is Green Professor at the University of Chicago Law School. He received the B.S. degree from the University of Kansas and the J.D. from the University of Chicago. He has been assistant director of the U.S. Office of Management and the Budget and executive director of the U.S. Council on Economic Policy. Professor Dam specializes in civil procedure, constitutional law, international organizations, antitrust, international law, and regulated industries.

Oliver Williamson is professor of economics and law at the University of Pennsylvania. He received the B.S. degree from M.I.T., the M.B.A. from Stanford University, and the Ph.D. from Carnegie-Mellon University. He has been special economic assistant in the Antitrust Division of the U.S. Department of Justice and has taught at the University of California as well as the University of Pennsylvania. Professor Williamson has published extensive research in antitrust, regulation, and the economics of the large corporation.

147

About the Editor

Robert D. Tollison is professor of economics at Virginia Polytechnic Institute and State University. He received the A.B. degree from Wofford College, the M.A. from the University of Alabama, and the Ph.D. from the University of Virginia. He is executive director of the Center for Public Choice at Virginia Polytechnic Institute and State University and has taught at Cornell University and Texas A&M University. Professor Tollison has published extensively in the fields of public finance, public choice, and industrial organization.